# Mental Health

# Other books in the Current Controversies series

*Current*
**CONTROVERSIES**

# Mental Health

*Ann Quigley, Book Editor*

**GREENHAVEN PRESS**
*An imprint of Thomson Gale, a part of The Thomson Corporation*

THOMSON
GALE™

Detroit • New York • San Francisco • New Haven, Conn. • Waterville, Maine • London

Christine Nasso, *Publisher*
Elizabeth Des Chenes, *Managing Editor*

© 2007 Thomson Gale, a part of The Thomson Corporation.

Thomson and Star logo are trademarks and Gale and Greenhaven Press are registered trademarks used herein under license.

*For more information, contact:*
Greenhaven Press
27500 Drake Rd.
Farmington Hills, MI 48331-3535
Or you can visit our Internet site at http://www.gale.com

LIBRARY OF CONGRESS CATALOGING-IN-PUBLICATION DATA

Mental health / Ann Quigley, book editor.
        p. cm. -- (Current controversies)
    Includes bibliographical references and index.
    ISBN-13: 978-0-7377-2484-4 (hardcover)
    ISBN-13: 978-0-7377-2485-1 (pbk.)
    1. Mental health. 2. Mental illness. I. Quigley, Ann.
    RA790.M3615 2007
    616.89--dc22

                                                                2007013238

ISBN-10: 0-7377-2484-6 (hardcover)
ISBN-10: 0-7377-2485-4 (pbk.)

Printed in the United States of America
10 9 8 7 6 5 4 3 2 1

# Contents

## Chapter 1: Is Mental Illness a Serious Problem in the United States?

*Benedict Carey*

Psychiatrists have no good answer to questions about where mental health ends and illness begins—and the boundary between these two states has become a battle line dividing the profession into two camps. On one side are doctors who say mental illness should include mild conditions that affect quality of life; on the other are experts who say definitions should be tightened so resources go to those who need them most.

### Yes: Mental Illness Is a Serious Problem

*William M. Welch*

Iraq War veterans are returning home with emotional as well as bodily scars—thousands are suffering from mental health disorders such as post-traumatic stress disorder (PTSD).

*Marianne Szegedy-Maszak*

The human cost of letting depression go untreated is massive, since not only can depression hinder the human pursuit of happiness, evidence is mounting that it may increase one's risk of diseases including heart disease, diabetes, and cancer. Nearly 25 percent of American women and 10 percent of American men will be clinically depressed at some point in their lives.

# Chapter 2: Are Drugs the Best Way to Treat Mental Illness?

**Yes: Drugs Help Treat Mental Illness**

**No: Drugs May Not Be the Best Way to Treat Mental Illness**

# Chapter 3: What Are Alternative Treatments for Mental Illness?

*Abby Ellin*

While it has long been known that exercise lifts the spirits of those without mental illness, experts increasingly recommend exercise for people with mental illness. It's been shown to improve the psychological health of those who suffer moderate depression, and now newer research is also finding it helpful for people with conditions like bipolar disorder, schizophrenia, and severe anxiety disorders.

The Economist

The largest clinical trial ever to compare talk therapy with antidepressants has found that talking works as well as taking pills—in fact it works better, if you factor in lower relapse rates. The study looked at a modern type of talk therapy called cognitive therapy, which trains people how to change negative thought patterns.

*Jody Jaffe*

A painless and noninvasive therapy known as neurofeedback training can essentially help to retrain brain waves. This approach can help treat disorders such as attention deficit/hyperactivity disorder, depression, and obsessive-compulsive disorder.

*David Servan-Schreiber*

It is now believed that some mental disorders may arise from stress-related inflammation in the brain. Scientists say that omega-3 fatty acids may serve as a sort of brain fuel that helps protect the brain from inflammation-induced damage—and give relief from the symptoms of mental disorders such as postpartum depression and bipolar disorder.

# Chapter 4: How Should Society Respond to the Mentally Ill?

# Foreword

By definition, controversies are "discussions of questions in which opposing opinions clash" (Webster's Twentieth Century Dictionary Unabridged). Few would deny that controversies are a pervasive part of the human condition and exist on virtually every level of human enterprise. Controversies transpire between individuals and among groups, within nations and between nations. Controversies supply the grist necessary for progress by providing challenges and challengers to the status quo. They also create atmospheres where strife and warfare can flourish. A world without controversies would be a peaceful world; but it also would be, by and large, static and prosaic.

## The Series' Purpose

The purpose of the Current Controversies series is to explore many of the social, political, and economic controversies dominating the national and international scenes today. Titles selected for inclusion in the series are highly focused and specific. For example, from the larger category of criminal justice, Current Controversies deals with specific topics such as police brutality, gun control, white collar crime, and others. The debates in Current Controversies also are presented in a useful, timeless fashion. Articles and book excerpts included in each title are selected if they contribute valuable, long-range ideas to the overall debate. And wherever possible, current information is enhanced with historical documents and other relevant materials. Thus, while individual titles are current in focus, every effort is made to ensure that they will not become quickly outdated. Books in the Current Controversies series will remain important resources for librarians, teachers, and students for many years.

In addition to keeping the titles focused and specific, great care is taken in the editorial format of each book in the series. Book introductions and chapter prefaces are offered to provide background material for readers. Chapters are organized around several key questions that are answered with diverse opinions representing all points on the political spectrum. Materials in each chapter include opinions in which authors clearly disagree as well as alternative opinions in which authors may agree on a broader issue but disagree on the possible solutions. In this way, the content of each volume in Current Controversies mirrors the mosaic of opinions encountered in society. Readers will quickly realize that there are many viable answers to these complex issues. By questioning each author's conclusions, students and casual readers can begin to develop the critical thinking skills so important to evaluating opinionated material.

Current Controversies is also ideal for controlled research. Each anthology in the series is composed of primary sources taken from a wide gamut of informational categories including periodicals, newspapers, books, U.S. and foreign government documents, and the publications of private and public organizations. Readers will find factual support for reports, debates, and research papers covering all areas of important issues. In addition, an annotated table of contents, an index, a book and periodical bibliography, and a list of organizations to contact are included in each book to expedite further research.

Perhaps more than ever before in history, people are confronted with diverse and contradictory information. During the Persian Gulf War, for example, the public was not only treated to minute-to-minute coverage of the war, it was also inundated with critiques of the coverage and countless analyses of the factors motivating U.S. involvement. Being able to sort through the plethora of opinions accompanying today's major issues, and to draw one's own conclusions, can be a complicated and frustrating struggle. It is the editors' hope that Current Controversies will help readers with this struggle.

# Introduction

In August of 2006 a prison inmate named Timothy Souders died of thirst in his segregation cell in Jackson, Michigan. Before he died, his hands, feet, and waist had been chained to a concrete slab for seventeen hours. Despite what these harsh conditions suggest, Souders wasn't a hardcore criminal. This twenty-one-year-old man suffered from manic depression and sometimes exhibited psychotic behavior. After he was caught shoplifting two paintball guns, Souders threatened employees with a pocketknife, and then begged a police officer to shoot him. Instead he was stunned with a Taser gun and sent to jail.

This scenario reflects America's tendency in recent years to cope with the mentally ill—when they exhibit even the smallest amount of aggressive behavior—via jails rather than hospitals. According to a study released by the Justice Department in 2006, more than half of inmates across the country reported mental health problems within the past year. "It should be clear why there is such a large proportion of mentally ill persons in our prisons," writes Bernard E. Harcourt, a professor of law and criminology at the University of Chicago, in a *New York Times* op-ed column. "Individuals who used to be tracked for mental health treatment are now getting a one-way ticket to jail." According to Harcourt, "we now incarcerate more than two million people—resulting in the highest incarceration number and rate in the world, five times that of Britain and twelve times that of Japan."

No one wants suffering individuals like Timothy Souders to die in jail, especially when effective drug and psychotherapy treatments exist to treat his illness. But a great deal of controversy surrounds the best way to do this. Some say it is the responsibility of state governments to help people like Souders, as they used to in the past. This approach is too expensive, say critics. During the last half-century, budget cuts closed state mental hospitals in state after state, as the United States dismantled a massive web of costly government-funded mental health services.

Some states are trying to reestablish programs lost to budget cuts. Oregon, for example, is trying to set up programs to help mentally ill people afford housing, pay for drug treatments, and get substance abuse counseling. But these community services are extremely costly. They account for most of a $113 million increase requested in the 2007–2009 budget by the state's Office of Mental Health and Addiction Services.

To cut costs, states across the country have privatized mental health care; that is, they refer patients to a network of private providers contracted by the state. This approach is known as managed care. Proponents of mental health managed care say that following a business model is the only way to keep mental health care cost effective. Critics say the managed care approach to mental health destroys the delicate safety net that a good community mental health system provides. Managed care companies are concerned only with the bottom line, say critics, and it is too easy for people like Timothy Souders to slip through the cracks.

The controversies surrounding mental health care illustrate the dynamic nature of society's perspectives on mental health. Far from being a static construct, society's view of mental health evolves over time—especially as science gleans more insights on the inner workings of the brain. The entire arena of mental health is a particularly fertile ground for discussion, and this anthology, *Current Controversies: Mental Health*, presents a range of contrasting opinions on mental health issues, including how mental illness should be defined, how it should be treated, and how modern society and the legal system should approach mental health issues.

# Is Mental Illness a Serious Problem in the United States?

# Overview: The Battle to Define Mental Illness

*Benedict Carey*

*Benedict Carey writes about behavior and psychology for the* New York Times *Science section.*

A college student becomes so compulsive about cleaning his dorm room that his grades begin to slip. An executive living in New York has a mortal fear of snakes but lives in Manhattan and rarely goes outside the city where he might encounter one. A computer technician, deeply anxious around strangers, avoids social and company gatherings and is passed over for promotion.

Are these people mentally ill?

In a [2005] report, researchers estimated that more than half of Americans would develop mental disorders in their lives, raising questions about where mental health ends and illness begins.

In fact, psychiatrists have no good answer, and the boundary between mental illness and normal mental struggle has become a battle line dividing the profession into two viscerally opposed camps.

On one side are doctors who say that the definition of mental illness should be broad enough to include mild conditions, which can make people miserable and often lead to more severe problems later.

On the other are experts who say that the current definitions should be tightened to ensure that limited resources go to those who need them the most and to preserve the profession's credibility with a public that often scoffs at claims that large numbers of Americans have mental disorders.

Benedict Carey, "Snake Phobias, Moodiness and a Battle in Psychiatry," *New York Times*, June 14, 2005. Copyright © 2005 The New York Times Company. Reprinted with permission.

The question is not just philosophical: where psychiatrists draw the line may determine not only the willingness of insurers to pay for services, but the future of research on moderate and mild mental disorders. Directly and indirectly, it will also shape the decisions of millions of people who agonize over whether they or their loved ones are in need of help, merely eccentric or dealing with ordinary life struggles.

"This argument is heating up right now," said Dr. Darrel Regier, director of research at the American Psychiatric Association, "because we're in the process of revising the diagnostic manual," the catalog of mental disorders on which research, treatment and the profession itself are based.

The next edition of the manual is expected to appear in 2010 or 2011, "and there's going [to be] continued debate in the scientific community about what the cut-points of clinical disease are," Dr. Regier said.

## An Intangible Illness

Psychiatrists have been searching for more than a century for some biological marker for mental disease, to little avail. Although there is promising work in genetics and brain imaging, researchers are not likely to have anything resembling a blood test for a mental illness soon, leaving them with what they have always had: observations of behavior, and patients' answers to questions about how they feel and how severe their condition is.

Severity is at the core of the debate. Are slumps in mood bad enough to make someone miss work? Does anxiety over social situations disrupt friendships and play havoc with romantic relationships?

Insurers have long incorporated severity measures in decisions about what to cover. Dr. Alex Rodriguez, chief medical officer for behavioral health at Magellan Health Services, the country's largest managed mental health insurer, said that Magellan used several standardized tests to rate how much a problem is interfering with someone's life. The company is developing its own scale to track how well people function. "This is a tool that would allow the therapist to monitor a patient's progress from session to session," he said.

Although the current edition of the American Psychiatric Association's catalog of mental disorders includes severity as a part of diagnosis, some experts say these measures are not tough or specific enough.

Dr. Stuart Kirk, a professor of social welfare at the University of California, Los Angeles, who has been critical of the manual, gives examples of what could, under the current diagnostic guidelines, qualify as a substance abuse disorder: a college student who every month or so drinks too much beer on Sunday night and misses his chemistry class at 8 a.m. Monday, lowering his grade; or a middle-aged professional who smokes a joint now and then drives to a restaurant, risking arrest.

"Although perhaps representing bad judgment," Dr. Kirk wrote in an e-mail message, these cases "would not be seen by most people as valid examples of mental illness, and they shouldn't be because they represent no underlying, internal, pathological mental state."

Separating the heavies from the lightweights—by asking, say, "Did you ever go to a doctor for your problem, or talk to anyone about it?"—has a significant effect on who counts as mentally impaired.

After researchers reported in a large national survey in 1994 that 30 percent of American adults had a mental illness in the past year, Dr. Regier and others reanalyzed the data, taking into account whether people had reported their mental troubles to a therapist or friend, had received treatment or had taken other actions.

They found that the number of people who qualified for a diagnosis of mental illness in the previous year plunged to 20 percent over all; rates of some disorders dropped by a third to half.

But limiting the count to those who have taken action does not give an accurate picture of the extent of illness, argue other researchers, who have been sharply critical of efforts to drive down prevalence estimates.

Dr. Robert Spitzer, a professor of psychiatry at Columbia University and the principal architect of the third edition of the diagnostic manual, wrote in a letter to The Archives of Psychiatry, "Many physical disorders are often transient and mild and may not require treatment (e.g. acute viral infections or low back syndrome). It would be absurd to recognize such conditions only when treatment was indicated."

He added, "Let us not revise diagnostic criteria that help us make clinically valid standard diagnoses in order to make community prevalence data easier to justify to a skeptical public."

## Mild Cases Are Important Too

Dr. Ronald Kessler, a professor of health care policy at Harvard . . . said squeezing diagnoses so that many mild cases drop out could blind the profession to a group of people it should be paying more attention to, not less.

"We know that there are prodromes, states that put people at higher risk, like hypertension for heart disease, which doctors treat," he said. "You can call these milder mental conditions what you want, and you may decide to treat them or not, but if you don't identify them they fall off the radar, and you don't know much of anything about them."

In the survey [released in 2005], Dr. Kessler and his colleagues found that half of disorders started by age 14, and three-quarters by age 24. "These are people who may show up at age 25 or later as depressed alcoholics, maybe they're in trouble with the law, they've lost relationships, and from my perspective we need to go upstream and find out what's happening before they become so desperate," Dr. Kessler said.

One condition whose estimated prevalence has bounced around like a Ping-Pong ball in this debate is social phobia, extreme anxiety over social situations. In a 1984 survey, investigators identified social phobia primarily by asking about excessive fear of speaking in public. They found a one-year prevalence rate of 1.7 percent.

---

*Only when he began badly mangling presentations at work, and then dreaded going in at all, did he tell his wife that he felt he was in trouble. His wife had watched a therapist talk about social phobia on television, and soon he was getting help.*

---

But psychiatrists soon concluded that other kinds of fears, including a fear of eating in public or using public restrooms, were variations of social phobia. When, in 1994, these and others questions were included, the prevalence rate rose to 7.4 percent.

Dr. Regier re-evaluated the data using a different criterion for severity and found a much lower rate: 3.2 percent. [In the 2005 report], Dr. Kessler reported a rate of 6.8 percent.

"You can see why people have a hard time believing these numbers because they change so much depending on how you look at the data," said Dr. David Mechanic, director of the Institute for Health, Health Care Policy and Aging Research at Rutgers University.

Yet the cutoff points for disease severity have real effects on the lives of people like Paul Pusateri, 48, a Baltimore business analyst.

Mr. Pusateri said he was outgoing through college but then had a panic attack in his mid-20's, as he was preparing to give a speech. He managed to build a career and family despite surges of anxiety before speeches and meetings. But finally, more than two decades after the first symptoms, he reached a point where he dreaded even small or one-on-one meetings with familiar co-workers.

---

*Despite increasing openness about mental illness the public tends to be skeptical of any prevalence numbers over a few percent.*

---

"It's very bizarre; the only way I can describe the feeling is, imagine walking down the street at dusk having someone put a gun in your face and threaten to kill you—having that absolute terror before a routine work meeting," he said.

Mr. Pusateri said that, perhaps unconsciously, he applied severity criteria to his own growing mental struggles. He may have set the bar too high: only when he began badly mangling presentations at work, and then dreaded going in at all, did he tell his wife that he felt he was in trouble. His wife had watched a therapist talk about social phobia on television, and soon he was getting help.

He considers himself lucky to have found a diagnosis at all, not to mention a therapist. "I was desperate by the time I did anything about it, I saw that my livelihood was at stake," he said.

Yet by all outside appearances, and by some strict definitions, he might not have qualified as having a disorder until he took some action.

## The Battle to Define Mental Illness

In the coming years, Dr. Regier's office will be responsible for clarifying the thresholds of disease for the next diagnostic manual, to somehow identify difficult cases like this one, while remaining credible to insurers and to the public at large.

After a prolonged controversy last year over the use of antidepressants in children, most experts say the last thing psychiatry needs now is for this process to turn into a public fight over who is sick and who is not.

But this fight may be hard to avoid. The two sides are far apart, debates over the diagnostic manual are traditionally contentious and despite increasing openness about mental illness the public tends to be skeptical of any prevalence numbers over a few percent.

"That's the problem," said Dr. Regier, "people hear these higher prevalence rates and they immediately start thinking about severe, disabling schizophrenia. But we know these surveys include a lot of mild cases, and we need to ask, How significant are these?"

# Post-traumatic Stress Disorder Is a Serious Problem for Iraq War Veterans

*William M. Welch*

*William M. Welch is a reporter for* USA Today.

Jeremy Harrison sees the warning signs in the Iraq war veterans who walk through his office door every day—flashbacks, inability to relax or relate, restless nights and more.

He recognizes them as symptoms of combat stress because he's trained to, as a counselor at the small storefront Vet Center here run by the U.S. Department of Veterans Affairs. He recognizes them as well because he, too, has faced readjustment in the year since he returned from Iraq, where he served as a sergeant in an engineering company that helped capture Baghdad in 2003.

"Sometimes these sessions are helpful to me," Harrison says, taking a break from counseling some of the nation's newest combat veterans. "Because I deal with a lot of the same problems."

As the United States [continues] its military presence in Iraq still fighting a violent insurgency, it is also coming to grips with one of the products of war at home: a new generation of veterans, some of them scarred in ways seen and unseen. While military hospitals mend the physical wounds, the VA is attempting to focus its massive health and benefits bureaucracy on the long-term needs of combat veterans after they leave military service. Some suffer from wounds of flesh and bone, others of emotions and psyche.

These injured and disabled men and women represent the most grievously wounded group of returning combat veterans since the Vietnam War, which officially ended in 1975. Of more than 5 million veterans treated at VA facilities last year, from counseling centers like this one to big hospitals, 48,733 were from the fighting in Iraq and Afghanistan.

Many of the most common wounds aren't seen until soldiers return home. Post-traumatic stress disorder, or PTSD, is an often-debilitating mental condition that can produce a range of unwanted emotional responses to the trauma of combat. It can emerge weeks, months or years later. If left untreated, it can severely affect the lives not only of veterans, but their families as well.

Of the 244,054 veterans of Iraq and Afghanistan already discharged from service, 12,422 have been in VA counseling centers for readjustment problems and symptoms associated with PTSD. Comparisons to past wars are difficult because emotional problems were often ignored or written off as "combat fatigue" or "shell shock." PTSD wasn't even an official diagnosis, accepted by the medical profession, until after Vietnam.

There is greater recognition of the mental-health consequences of combat now, and much research has been done in the past 25 years. The VA has a program that attempts to address them and supports extensive research. Harrison is one of 50 veterans of the Iraq and Afghanistan wars hired by the VA as counselors for their fellow veterans.

## Reliving the Horror

Post-traumatic stress was defined in 1980, partly based on the experiences of soldiers and victims of war. It produces a wide range of symptoms in men and women who have experienced a traumatic event that provoked intense fear, helplessness or horror.

The events are sometimes re-experienced later through intrusive memories, nightmares, hallucinations or flashbacks, usually triggered by anything that symbolizes or resembles the trauma. Troubled sleep, irritability, anger, poor concentration, hypervigilance and exaggerated responses are often symptoms.

Individuals may feel depression, detachment or estrangement, guilt, intense anxiety and panic, and other negative emotions. They often feel they have little in common with civilian peers; issues that concern friends and family seem trivial after combat.

Harrison says they may even hit their partners during nightmares and never know it.

Many Iraq veterans have returned home to find the aftermath of combat presents them with new challenges:

Jesus Bocanegra was an Army infantry scout for units that pursued Saddam Hussein in his hometown of Tikrit. After he returned home to McAllen, Texas, it took him six months to find a job.

He was diagnosed with PTSD and is waiting for the VA to process his disability claim. He goes to the local Vet Center but is unable to relate to the Vietnam-era counselors.

"I had real bad flashbacks. I couldn't control them," Bocanegra, 23, says. "I saw the murder of children, women. It was just horrible for anyone to experience."

---

*The smell of diesel would trigger things for me. Loud noises, crowds, heavy traffic give me a hard time now. I have a lot of panic.... You feel like you're choking.*

---

Bocanegra recalls calling in Apache helicopter strikes on a house by the Tigris River where he had seen crates of enemy ammunition carried in. When the gunfire ended, there was silence.

But then children's cries and screams drifted from the destroyed home, he says. "I didn't know there were kids there," he says. "Those screams are the most horrible thing you can hear."

At home in the Rio Grande Valley, on the Mexico border, he says young people have no concept of what he's experienced. His readjustment has been difficult: His friends threw a homecoming party for him, and he got arrested for drunken driving on the way home.

"The Army is the gateway to get away from poverty here," Bocanegra says. "You go to the Army and expect to be better off, but the best job you can get (back home) is flipping burgers. . . . What am I supposed to do now? How are you going to live?"

Lt. Julian Goodrum, an Army reservist from Knoxville, Tenn., is being treated for PTSD with therapy and anti-anxiety drugs at Walter Reed Army Medical Center in Washington. He checked himself into a civilian psychiatric hospital after he was turned away from a military clinic, where he had sought attention for his mental problems at Fort Knox, Ky. He's facing a court-martial for being AWOL while in the civilian facility.

Goodrum, 34, was a transportation platoon leader in Iraq, running convoys of supplies from Kuwait into Iraq during the invasion. He returned to the USA in the summer of 2003 and experienced isolation, depression, an inability to sleep and racing thoughts.

"It just accumulated until it overwhelmed me. I was having a breakdown and trying to get assistance," he says. "The smell of diesel would trigger things for me. Loud noises, crowds, heavy traffic give me a hard time now. I have a lot of panic. . . . You feel like you're choking."

Sean Huze, a Marine corporal awaiting discharge at Camp Lejeune, N.C., doesn't have PTSD but says everyone who saw combat suffers from at least some combat stress. He says the unrelenting insurgent threat in Iraq gives no opportunity to relax, and combat numbs the senses and emotions.

"There is no 'front,'" Huze says. "You go back to the rear, at the Army base in Mosul, and you go in to get your chow, and the chow hall blows up."

Huze, 30, says the horror often isn't felt until later. "I saw a dead child, probably 3 or 4 years old, lying on the road in Nasiriyah," he says. "It moved me less than if I saw a dead dog at the time. I didn't care. Then you come back, if you are fortunate enough, and hold your own child, and you think of the dead child you didn't care about. . . . You think about how little you cared at the time, and that hurts."

Smells bring back the horror. "A barbecue pit—throw a steak on the grill, and it smells a lot like searing flesh," he says. "You go to get your car worked on, and if anyone is welding, the smell of the burning metal is no different than burning caused by rounds fired at it. It takes you back there instantly."

---

*Soldiers and Marines who need counseling the most are least likely to seek it because of the stigma of mental health care in the military.*

---

Allen Walsh, an Army reservist, came back to Tucson 45 pounds lighter and with an injured wrist. He was unable to get his old job back teaching at a truck-driving school. He started his own business instead, a mobile barbecue service. He's been waiting nearly a year on a disability claim with the VA.

Walsh, 36, spent much of the war in Kuwait, attached to a Marine unit providing force protection and chemical decontamination. He says he has experienced PTSD, which he attributes to the constant threat of attack and demand for instant life-or-death decisions.

"It seemed like every day you were always pointing your weapon at somebody. It's something I have to live with," he says.

At home, he found he couldn't sleep more than three or four hours a night. When the nightmares began, he started smoking cigarettes. He'd find himself shaking and quick-tempered.

"Any little noise and I'd jump out of bed and run around the house with a gun," he says. "I'd wake up at night with cold sweats."

## 'A Safe Environment'

A recent Defense Department study of combat troops returning from Iraq found that soldiers and Marines who need counseling the most are least likely to seek it because of the stigma of mental health care in the military.

One in six troops questioned in the study admitted to symptoms of severe depression, PTSD or other problems. Of those, six in 10 felt their commanders would treat them differently and fellow troops would lose confidence if they acknowledged their problems.

*For them, this is the only chance to talk to somebody, because their families don't understand, their friends don't understand.*

A [2005] report by the Government Accountability Office said the VA "is a world leader in PTSD treatment." But it said the department "does not have sufficient capacity to meet the needs of new combat veterans while still providing for veterans of past wars." It said the department hasn't met its own goals for PTSD clinical care and education, even as it anticipates "greater numbers of veterans with PTSD seeking VA services."

Harrison, who was a school counselor and Army Reservist from Wheeling, W.Va., before being called to active duty in January 2003, thinks cases of PTSD may be even more common than the military's one-in-six estimate.

He is on the leading edge of the effort to help these veterans back home. Harrison and other counselors invite Iraq and Afghanistan veterans to stop in to talk. Often, that leads to counseling sessions and regular weekly group therapy. If appropriate, they refer the veterans to VA doctors for drug therapies such as antidepressants and anti-anxiety medications.

## Vets Learn They Are Not Alone

"First of all, I let them talk. I want to find out all their problems," he says. "Then I assure them they're not alone. It's OK."

Fifty counselors from the latest war is a small number, considering the VA operates 206 counseling centers across the country. Their strategy is to talk with veterans about readjustment before they have problems, or before small problems become big ones. The VA also has staff at 136 U.S. military bases now, including five people at Walter Reed, where many of the most grievously injured are sent.

The toughest part of helping veterans, Harrison says, is getting them to overcome fears of being stigmatized and to step into a Vet Center. "They think they can handle the situation themselves," he says.

Vet Centers provide help for broader issues of readjustment back to civilian life, including finding a job, alcohol and drug abuse counseling, sexual trauma counseling, spouse and family counseling, and mental or emotional problems that fall short of PTSD.

More than 80% of the staff are veterans, and 60% served in combat zones, says Al Batres, head of the VA's readjustment counseling service. "We're oriented toward peer counseling, and we provide a safe environment for soldiers who have been traumatized," he says.

"A Vietnam veteran myself, it would have been so great if we'd had this kind of outreach," says Johnny Bragg, director of the Vet Center where Harrison works. "If you can get with the guys who come back fresh ... and actually work with their trauma and issues, hopefully over the years you won't see the long-term PTSD."

In all cases, the veteran has to be the one who wants to talk before counselors can help. "Once they come through the door, they usually come back," Harrison says. "For them, this is the only chance to talk to somebody, because their families don't understand, their friends don't understand. That's the big thing. They can't talk to anyone. They can't relate to anyone."

# Depression Takes a Serious Toll on Physical as Well as Mental Health

*Marianne Szegedy-Maszak*

*Marianne Szegedy-Maszak is a senior writer at* U.S. News & World Report *and a contributing writer to the* Los Angeles Times.

Bryce Miller's work as an industrial engineer in Topeka, Kan., wasn't a whole lot more challenging than the job he faces in retirement: engineering his own medical care by 10 different doctors. Miller, 74, sees a team of specialists, which includes a cardiologist, a urologist and radiologist for prostate cancer, an endocrinologist for diabetes, a nephrologist for kidney problems, and a psychiatrist to manage the severe episodes of depression he has suffered during a long struggle with bipolar disorder. "I can't find a doctor who can handle all of it," he says.

It's impossible to pinpoint all the causes of Miller's illness; a combination of bad genes, bad luck, and bad diet probably gets much of the blame. But lately, he says, he's been wondering whether his mental state may have played a role, too. Medicine has recognized for some time that chronically sick people are prone to depression and that those affected have a tougher road back. Now, the signs are mounting that the spectrum of depressive illness, and perhaps even bitter loneliness, may actually make healthy people more vulnerable to a range of physical ailments. "There is a growing body of evidence suggesting that depression might be a causal risk factor in diseases like ischemic heart disease, stroke, diabetes, and immune-based diseases like cancer and HIV/AIDS," says

Dwight Evans, chair of psychiatry at the University of Pennsylvania medical school. "And there is also considerable recent evidence that mood disorders can affect the course of medical illnesses. It goes both ways. Depression may be both a cause and a consequence of medical illness."

## Depression as a Risk Factor

Consider a study published last month in the journal *Diabetologia*, which concluded that depressed adults have a 37 percent greater risk' of developing type 2 diabetes than the rest of the population; other studies have suggested their risk actually doubles. (Apparently, English physician Thomas Willis was on to something when he wrote in 1674, "Diabetes is caused by melancholy.") One intriguing recent study of Alzheimer's patients revealed that those with a history of depression had more extensive plaques in their brains. Depressed postmenopausal women with no history of heart disease are much more likely to develop it and die of it than their peers. In March, University of Chicago researchers showed that loneliness can spike blood pressure by 30 points in older people. Pancreatic cancer, for reasons scientists don't understand, is often preceded by a serious depression before the disease asserts itself.

And when melancholy comes on the heels of disease, it appears to compound the physical insult. Diabetes is more likely to be uncontrolled, for example. And several studies have found that in the months right after a heart attack, the depressed patients are much more likely to die than the others.

If the researchers are right, the human cost of letting depression go untreated is staggering. Nearly 25 percent of American women and 10 percent of men will be clinically depressed at some point in their lives; a massive study conducted by the World Health Organization, Harvard University School of Public Health, and the World Bank found that by

2020, depression will be second only to heart disease as a cause of medical and physical disability. . . .

What might explain the mind's influence on physical health? Certainly, chronic depression does not encourage a healthy lifestyle. "Depressed individuals don't exercise. They are more likely not to take medication, and it is harder for them to lose weight and stop smoking," says Nancy Frasure-Smith, a professor of psychiatry at the University of Montreal and McGill University who has long studied the link between depression and cardiovascular disease.

## The Biochemistry of Depression

But depression also acts on the body's systems in ways scientists are only beginning to understand. Extra stress hormones are produced, for example—along with chemicals that trigger inflammation. When the hormone cortisol is secreted in response to stress, the body's blood glucose level rises to provide a burst of energy. A depressed brain's constant signal that it's under stress and needs more energy complicates the body's regulation of blood sugar. Might this explain why depression seems to both trigger and exacerbate diabetes?

---

*When they stuck my finger 15 years ago and found out that I was diabetic, it never occurred to me that my depression had something to do with it. . . . But now it just seems so clear: The brain is always connected with the body.*

---

A stress response may set depressed people up for cardiovascular disease, too—or aggravate it. When the blood-clotting system gets ready for impending injury, sticky cells called platelets go on high alert to slow down bleeding. In depressed people, one study showed, the platelets are more apt to be in this state of readiness. The problem: Clotting is what causes heart attacks and strokes. Chemicals called cytokines flood the bloodstream, as well. These messengers from the immune system cause inflammation, which makes blood vessels thicken and artery-hardening plaques form.

Researchers have also noted another stress reaction: The heart muscles of depressed patients lose flexibility. A normal heart transitions easily between its resting and beating states; more rigid muscle is less able to respond to the changing demands of the body for blood and oxygen. A study published [in March 2006] in the *Journal of the American College of Cardiology* found that mental stress caused a more dramatic decrease in blood flow to the heart muscle—or ischemia—than a stress test on a treadmill. All told, stress and depression probably explain "close to 30 percent of the total risk of heart attacks," estimates David Sheps, professor of medicine and associate chief of cardiovascular medicine at the University of Florida.

## More Research Is Needed

It's way too soon to make the leap that depression is a direct cause of heart disease akin to smoking or high cholesterol, or that treatment—like quitting cigarettes—can reverse the damage or save lives. . . .

What . . . seems certain, however mysterious all these connections may be, is that mental health can no longer be considered a separate issue. Realizing that there may be links between his mental and physical illness has brought Bryce Miller some peace with a body that has often confused him. "When they stuck my finger 15 years ago and found out that I was diabetic, it never occurred to me that my depression had something to do with it," he says. "But now it just seems so clear: The brain is always connected to the body."

# Teen Mental Illness
# Is a Serious Problem

*Jeff Q. Bostic and Michael Craig Miller*

*Jeff Q. Bostic is director of school psychiatry at Massachusetts General Hospital and an assistant professor of psychiatry at Harvard Medical School. Michael Craig Miller is editor in chief of the* Harvard Mental Health Letter.

He sleeps the day away, and is irritable when he's awake. She's moody and mopes around. He eats everything or almost nothing. She hides in her room, shunning even the simplest chores. Does this sound like a teenager you know?

Neuroscientists suspect the adolescent brain is wired for emotional turbulence and retreat from the family. These tendencies may help teenagers separate from their parents and reach out to peers. But those same tendencies can make it hard to tell when the work of growing up is turning into a depression that deserves treatment. Roughly one out of 12 teens suffers significant depression before the age of 18. Girls, once they reach puberty, are twice as likely as boys to become depressed. Approximately half of the teenagers with untreated depression may attempt suicide, which remains the third leading cause of death in this age group.

Important differences separate the growing pains of adolescence from depression. A painful breakup, a rejection by peers, a bad grade or a humiliating disagreement with an adult may cause unhappiness or frustration for a few days. Depression dominates life for weeks or months, and may appear for no known reason. Depressed kids—who may be biologically more vulnerable than others to environmental stress—feel almost constantly miserable and enjoy very little. But depression isn't always expressed as sadness. The teen may be irritable, or complain of headaches or stomach pains instead of describing a bad mood. Energy, sleep and appetite may suffer. Some depressed kids function poorly at school or withdraw from friends and family. And while it is normal for adolescents to think about mortality and the meaning of life, it's not normal to be preoccupied with death or to seriously contemplate suicide.

## Treating Teen Depression

Antidepressants are neither panacea nor poison, but they do help many kids. The worries about these drugs are famous. Right after starting an antidepressant, some kids do become more anxious or restless, and a few may have an increase in suicidal thoughts. But depression itself carries greater risks. It is much more likely to cause suicide, and it can thwart healthy development. Any teen starting anti-depressant therapy should be seen regularly by the prescribing doctor, and the family should call immediately if the child gets worse instead of better.

Medications are only part of good treatment, though. The measures that promote healthy adolescent growth also are helpful for depression. Moderate aerobic exercise relieved depressive symptoms in almost half of young adults in one recent study. Good sleeping and eating habits, while sometimes a tough sell to adolescents, can also improve mood. Psychotherapy can help teens figure out what makes them feel helpless or self-critical and develop strategies to put things right. And when adolescents latch on to an activity they value that also helps others, their mood improves, and so does their sense of self. Imaging studies confirm that altruistic behavior lights up the brain's reward areas.

The future may bring better antidepressants, along with better tools for identifying which medications are best suited to which child. But it's already possible for teens to learn to sustain relationships, to turn back thoughts that spur depression and to contribute to causes larger than themselves. By supporting them in these quests, we can ease the transition out of childhood, and help them build more fulfilling lives as adults.

# Mental Illness Is Overestimated in America

*Paul McHugh*

*Paul McHugh is a university distinguished service professor of psychiatry and behavioral science at the Johns Hopkins School of Medicine and former psychiatrist in chief of the Johns Hopkins Hospital.*

Psychiatric epidemiologists from the Harvard Medical School have published studies purporting to demonstrate that some 55 percent of Americans suffer from mental illness in their lifetime. These studies—which cost $20 million, most of it out of the taxpayer's pocket—were based on a survey of 9,282 randomly selected English-speaking subjects over the age of 18 who were seen in their homes by technicians trained to ask specific questions about symptoms believed to indicate mental illnesses. The results led Thomas Insel, director of the National Institute of Mental Health, the studies' primary sponsor, to note that indeed "mental disorders are highly prevalent and chronic." More than half the people of the United States, in other words, have been or are mentally ill. What should we make of this?

Not to put too fine a point on it, we should take the study's conclusions with a huge grain—perhaps a silo would be required—of salt. Diagnostic exaggeration dogs psychiatry today and will not subside until research psychiatrists use ways closer to those of practicing clinicians for recognizing mental disorders and differentiating the serious from the trivial in mental life. Let me explain.

The survey technicians were instructed to fill in a questionnaire by asking the subjects about mental symptoms such as depression and anxiety that they might have experienced in their lives. Such technicians, sticking to the prescribed inventory, essentially act as secretaries, recording what people say they recall from their past. The techs gather no sense of the persons they are meeting—no appreciation of their life circumstances, the issues they have dealt with, what strengths they brought to bear, or what vulnerabilities they overcame, in dealing with the good and bad fortune life brought them. The individual's family, social circumstances, temperament, character, opportunities, successes, and disappointments are all outside the attention of these interrogators.

Instead, the technicians run down their checklist of symptoms with no thought to causes, simply recording a yes or no answer to each. This is not a psychiatric examination; it is barely a census. The assessment does not rest on a trusting relationship, it presumes honesty and openness in the replies, and it assumes that both the subjects and the technicians understand the questions the same way the experts who constructed the inventory did. Finally, by focusing solely on symptoms—indications of disease or disorder—these inventories tend to direct attention to human frailty rather than to human strengths and to emphasize the burdens and obscure the gifts that life has brought these subjects. . . .

## Diagnosing with a Checklist

In addition to relying solely on respondents' yes or no answers to a checklist, the investigators are committed to employing the official Diagnostic and Statistical Manual of Mental Disorders—Fourth Edition (abbreviated DSM-IV), which bases all psychiatric diagnoses on symptoms and their course, not on any fuller knowledge of the person. It is as if public health investigators studying the prevalence of pneumonia over time in the American population were satisfied to call every instance of a cough with a fever and a mucoid sputum a case of pneumonia.

Internal medicine gave up on symptom-based diagnosis more than a hundred years ago, replacing it with diagnosis that rests on knowledge of pathology and what produces it. Thus, internists no longer speak of coughs as racking, brassy, or productive, but as produced by viral or bacterial infection, allergies, or vascular congestion. They no longer differentiate Tertian, Quotidian, and Continuous Fevers but fevers from infection, neoplasia, dehydration, and so on.

DSM-IV makes no attempt to classify mental symptoms or complaints by cause. As a result, it mingles serious and impairing conditions with other forms of mental distress in one hopeless and scientifically indigestible stew. When this diagnostic method is employed for a census of mental disorders in the citizenry, it ominously exaggerates the incidence and the nature of mental troubles. It leaves the public wondering: If more than 50 percent of Americans have at some point been mentally "impaired," what constitutes a "normal" mental life?

Another way of stating the problem is that DSM-IV is the medical counterpart of a naturalist's field guide—say, Roger Tory Peterson's Field Guide to the Birds. To develop his guide, Peterson asked expert bird watchers what features of shape, coloring, voice, and range they used to distinguish one warbler from another, and he arranged his guidebook accordingly. As a result, bird watchers became more precise in the terms they used to describe what they saw. But as Peterson noted, amateurs relying on the way birds look often confuse varieties with separate species, while ornithologists turn to biology to make more fundamental distinctions.

Similarly, clinical psychiatrists in 1980 wanted to find a way to apply their diagnostic terms consistently. With DSM-IV, they agreed on which symptoms they would use as criteria for each diagnosis, and thus increased their diagnostic consistency. But the best clinicians apply DSM-IV diagnostic terms only after they have fully examined the patient and come to see these symptoms in context. They do not simply run down a checklist of symptoms, count them up, and attach a diagnosis, as did the technicians from Harvard.

---

*With these more specific studies we would likely discover not that the majority of people are impaired but just how remarkably resilient most of us are and what distinct and wonderful assets most people bring to life.*

---

Psychiatrists are right now rewriting the diagnostic manual. I believe they will move closer to internal medicine, classifying patients according to what has provoked their symptoms rather than according to the symptoms alone. Only then will scientific and epidemiologic studies in psychiatry improve.

In the meantime, while scientists are working to lift psychiatry beyond the level of a field guide, epidemiologists should stop expending time and money repeating surveys that purport to measure the prevalence of psychiatric disorders but instead only mislead and alarm the public. They should spend their efforts in more productive areas of psychiatric research.

They might, for example, start following people over time, as cohorts with particular life circumstances: They might consider the long-term performance of children with particular classroom-identified dispositions or children exposed to various forms of deprivation or trauma early in life, seeking to discover how these people manage the hurdles they face and which vulnerabilities to mental problems and which resiliencies they manifest in later life. Epidemiologists should attend to studies where patients with particular characteristics—such as temperament, upbringing, or stress—are compared with nonpatients with similar characteristics (so called case-control studies) testing whether these characteristics provoke, protect against, or are incidental to the patients' mental unrest or illness. They should enhance cross-cultural knowledge of how mental impairment, as opposed to mental distress, is expressed by people of differing cultures and exactly what measures help to prevent or treat the case examples.

Analytic studies like these could accomplish much more than descriptive surveys that do little in the long run but exasperate the public and make ephemeral headlines. Along the way, with these more specific studies we would likely discover not that the majority of people are impaired but just how remarkably resilient most of us are and what distinct and wonderful assets most people bring to life. To conduct more of the same kind of empty surveys as are now being done is, I'm afraid, a little crazy—with crazy defined as doing the same thing again and again and expecting a different result.

# Mental Illness Is Too Broadly Defined

*Ashley Pettus*

*Ashley Pettus is a writer based in Cambridge, Massachusetts.*

By the time he reached his early thirties, James was a promising scientist who had all the makings of an academic star. He had earned a stream of fellowships and was on the path to tenure at one of Boston's preeminent universities. But James had a problem: he dreaded speaking in public. Academic conferences terrified him, so he avoided them whenever possible. He rarely interacted with colleagues. As a result, his ideas didn't circulate and his career stalled.

In frustration, James sought help from a psychiatrist, who diagnosed him with a mental disorder known as "social phobia" and prescribed a well-known antidepressant effective in the treatment of extreme inhibition. The medication alleviated his severe anxiety and enabled him to do the things he previously couldn't do. His work gained public recognition, and he has subsequently risen to the top of his profession.

In recent years, James's story has become increasingly common. Using an ever-expanding arsenal of neurochemical drugs, physicians now treat variants of mood and temperament that previous generations viewed as an inescapable part of life. In an earlier era, James's fears might have forced him to change professions. Today, the exceptionally shy and the overly anxious, the hyperactive and the chronically unhappy can seek relief from their suffering through medical intervention. And the parameters of what constitutes a "mental disorder" have swelled. An estimated 22 million Americans currently take psychotropic medications—most for relatively mild conditions.

Ashley Pettus, "Psychiatry by Prescription," *Harvard Magazine*, July–August 2006. Reproduced by permission of the author.

This widespread embrace of biological remedies to life's problems raises troubling questions for psychiatry. Paradoxically, even though psychopharmaceutical sales have soared in the United States during the past 20 years, only half of those with severe disorders receive adequate treatment. Clinicians and researchers disagree over what the priorities of the field should be and whom they should count as mentally ill. Are we over-treating the normal at the expense of the truly disturbed? Can we adequately distinguish illness from idiosyncrasy, disease from discontent? And are we allowing pharmaceutical companies and insurers to define the boundary between illness and health?

## The Slippery Slope of Diagnosis

A recent survey estimated that nearly half of all Americans will suffer a mental illness during their lifetimes. Harvard Medical School professor of health policy Ronald Kessler headed the two-year study, which polled 9,000 adults across the country, varying in age, education level, and marital status. Researchers conducted home-based, face-to-face interviews, using the World Health Organization's (WHO) diagnostic mental-health survey. They found that 29 percent of people experience some form of anxiety disorder, closely followed by impulse-control disorders (25 percent) and mood disorders (20 percent). Most cases begin in adolescence or early adulthood, and often, more than one disorder will strike simultaneously.

---

*If you haven't worked directly with people who suffer from so-called mild disorders, it's easy to write them off as ordinary.*

---

The study has sparked heated controversy. Critics argue that the numbers reflect a gross inflation of the meaning of "disease" that blurs the line between "real" disorders and normal forms of emotional and mental suffering. "By medicalizing ordinary unhappiness," says professor of psychiatry and medical anthropology Arthur Kleinman, who is also Rabb professor of anthropology, "we risk doing a disservice to those people who have severe mental illnesses." Kleinman fears that including mild forms of anxiety and depression under an ever-widening umbrella of mental disorders will divert attention and resources from diseases like schizophrenia and major depression, which remain undertreated and stigmatized across much of the world. In his view, "We may turn off the public, who are a huge source of support for mental-health research, by telling them that half of them are mad."

Kessler dismisses Kleinman's criticism as the "false enthusiasm of the noncombatant"—by which he means that if you haven't worked directly with people who suffer from so-called mild disorders, it's easy to write them off as ordinary. (Kleinman has been involved in developing global mental-health policy and programs with WHO; much of his research has focused on the cross-cultural study of mental illnesses such as schizophrenia and depression.) "Social phobia can be extremely debilitating," Kessler explains. "There are people who have absolutely no friends, no support system. Their lives are incredibly small and solitary. Many say they would rather have cancer." He points out that common mood and anxiety disorders also exact an enormous social burden in terms of days missed from work, cost to employers, and, in the worst cases, suicide. By contrast, he says, schizophrenia affects just 1 percent of the population.

At the heart of a debate over epidemiological statistics are deep misgivings about the way psychiatry defines and measures mental illness. Despite major advances in the treatment of psychiatric symptoms in recent years, there are still no definitive clinical tests to determine whether someone has a given disorder or not. "We have no equivalent of a blood-pressure cuff or blood test or brain scan that is diagnostic," says University provost Steven E. Hyman, professor of neuro-biology and the former director of the National Institute of Mental Health. The genetics of mental illness are also "fiend-ishly complex," he says; although there is evidence that many conditions run in families, science has yet to identify the par-ticular genes responsible for any disorder.

## Using Superficial Means to Diagnose Nuanced Disorders

Without clear biological markers, researchers and clinicians must rely on interviews to assess the occurrence and severity of mental disorders. Interview questions follow criteria from the *Diagnostic and Statistical Manual of Mental Disorders (DSM)*—a 1,000-page volume covering the gamut of human affect and behavior, from mood and personality to sexuality and addiction. Researchers have arrived at the syndromes listed in the *DSM* by tracking symptoms and symptom clus-ters, with particular attention to duration, age of onset, family prevalence, gender distribution, and response to treatment. Now in its revised fourth edition, the *DSM* has provided the field with a common language for identifying and discussing the enormous range of mental-health problems, yet it remains more a proximate description than a verifiable picture of real-ity.

---

*Milder disorders of mood and anxiety can share symp-toms with ordinary reactions to life events.*

---

"The *DSM* has given us reliability, meaning that—armed with the *DSM* criteria—two different observers should arrive at the same diagnosis in the same person," says Hyman. "But it has not given us validity." That is, one can't be sure that the various named disorders identify distinct syndromes in the brain. In the case of personality disorders, for instance, "If you get one diagnosis, you're likely to get two or three or five," Hyman points out. Similarly, people with depression often suffer from anxiety as well. "The proliferation of disorders in a single person," he says, "suggests there is something wrong with the number of discrete diagnoses."

This uncertainty at the core of psychiatry creates a slippery diagnostic slope. Severe illnesses, such as schizophrenia and major depression, tend to present relatively clear signs (delusions, hallucinations, catatonia, psychomotor problems). But milder disorders of mood and anxiety can share symptoms with ordinary reactions to life events. Kleinman contends that the high mental-illness rates recorded by Kessler reflect an over-reliance on a survey methodology that ignores the limitations of the science. "Lacking any laboratory tests," he says, "there's a tendency to let everything hang on questionnaires that researchers can even administer by telephone, using superficial questions and simple terms that can confuse the borderline between the normal and the abnormal."

Kleinman believes the weaknesses of psychiatric measurement are detrimental not only to the severely mentally ill, but also to the rest of us. The expansion of illness categories, he says, risks turning the most profound human experiences into medical problems. Grief over the loss of a loved one, or sadness in the face of death, for example, can look like depressive disorder, according to a checklist of *DSM* criteria. Doctors now routinely prescribe antidepressants to terminal patients on cancer wards and to bereaved family members whose grief symptoms persist beyond the *DSM's* "normal" two-month period. By making the emotions that accompany loss and dying into disease, Kleinman says, we are in danger as a society of flattening out our moral life. "The intent may be: why should anyone have to feel any degree of suffering?" he says. "And the result may be: if you make it difficult for people to engage suffering, you may actually change the nature of the world we live in." (He takes up these issues in a new book, *What Really Matters: Living a Moral Life Amidst Uncertainty and Danger.*)

Kessler and others involved in the measurement of mental disorders argue, on the other hand, that the advantage of catching cases early far outweighs the danger of over-counting. They compare mental illness to other medical markers, like blood pressure and cholesterol, for which definitions of disease are relative rather than absolute. As associate professor of psychiatry James Hudson, the director of the psychiatric epidemiology research program at McLean Hospital, points out, "The definition of 'high' blood pressure changes about every five years. Researchers come to an agreed-upon number by seeing that above a certain pressure there are more likely to be negative outcomes in terms of poor health. The blood pressure itself is not a disease, but a marker of risk." Depression and anxiety, Kessler says, similarly exist along a gradient: "The question is where on the spectrum a person starts tipping toward bad outcomes, such as isolation, job loss, or suicide."

Given the subjective nature of psychiatric diagnosis, determining the tipping point for mental illness is trickier than for purely physical conditions. Here the influence of drugs has been decisive. The introduction of relatively safe and effective psychotropic drugs like fluoxetine (Prozac, manufactured by Lilly), which can treat a range of psychiatric symptoms with few side effects, has increased the rate of diagnosis for many of the milder mood and anxiety disorders. "There is no such thing as 'real' depression," Kessler says. "The question is: are the symptoms clinically significant enough to treat? The answer depends on whether we have a clinically effective way of treating it."

Chemical remedies thus play a role in measuring and defining mental disorders. But skeptics warn that if clinicians' mere ability to treat symptoms identifies something as illness, disease categories will continue to expand while doctors' understanding of *what* they are treating will remain imprecise.

## Is Fear a Disease?

These concerns have flared over the diagnosis of "social phobia" (also called "social anxiety disorder"), which in just two decades has gone from "rare" (as listed in the *DSM-III*) to "common" (according to Kessler's national statistics). Critics believe that aggressive marketing by GlaxoSmithKline of its drug Paxil, an antidepressant effective in the treatment of shyness, has inflated the category. "Ten years ago, psychiatrists might see two or three cases of social phobia a year," says Joseph Glenmullen, a clinical instructor in psychiatry and a staff psychiatrist at Harvard Health Services. "These were people who were afraid to go to a movie because they were afraid of drawing attention to themselves if they had to get up to use the bathroom. They were terrified they wouldn't be able to get to the exit quickly enough." Since then, the condition has become ubiquitous. In 2001, the National Institute of Mental Health estimated that some five million American adults (nearly 4 percent of the adult population) suffer from social anxiety disorder. Diagnostic questions from national surveys identify symptoms that could apply to nearly anyone, such as: "Did you ever feel shy, afraid, or uncomfortable. . .meeting new people? Speaking up at a meeting? Giving a talk in front of an audience? Being in a dating situation?"

---

*Critics question whether intense shyness and fear of public speaking are signs of pathology or simply a disadvantageous personality trait.*

---

Clinicians who specialize in social anxiety emphasize the damage the disorder can inflict on lives. Associate professor of psychiatry Mark Pollack, director of the Center for Anxiety and Traumatic Stress Disorders at Massachusetts General Hospital, says that one of the hallmarks of social phobia is that people will make decisions about their careers based on their fears of interacting with new people or standing up in front of an audience. Many sufferers have struggled with anxiety since early adolescence, he says, but never thought they could do anything to change it. "Maybe they start having problems raising their hand in class. And if it makes them anxious to get up in front of a group, it's going to affect how they interview for college and it could even affect their willingness to go to college," he says. "So it can have an impact on their educational attainment and their ability to make a living."

Critics question whether intense shyness and fear of public speaking are signs of pathology or simply a disadvantageous personality trait. Many occupations today require public speaking, but "this does not make natural fear of such activities a disorder," a commentator in the *Canadian Journal of Psychiatry* points out, "any more than the fact that few people are smart enough to be physicists, tall enough to be basketball players, or beautiful enough to be models makes the rest of us disordered."

The groundbreaking work of developmental psychologist Jerome Kagan, Starch professor of psychology emeritus, has shown that humans inherit certain temperamental dispositions. Kagan demonstrated that 15 percent of infants are "high reactive"—that is, electroencephalograph tests show activation of the amygdala, indicating distress, when these babies encounter unfamiliar people or things. Depending on environmental conditions, some of these innately tense children, Kagan argues, will grow into socially anxious adults, while others may overcome fear of strangers but retain anxiety to other stimuli.

Kagan's work on innate temperament has bolstered research into the organic basis of social phobia and other anxiety conditions. But in recent years, Kagan himself has questioned a diagnostic approach that, he believes, formulaically equates impairing symptoms with a biological condition warranting medical treatment. "To say that 28 percent of Americans have anxiety disorders," he says, referring to Kessler's recent study, "assumes that being anxious is like having cancer. But anxiety is part of being human."

# Drug Makers Find New Markets by Publicizing "Hidden Epidemics" of Mental Illness

*Brendan I. Koerner*

*Brendan I. Koerner is a contributing editor at* Wired *and a fellow at the New American Foundation.*

Word of the hidden epidemic began spreading in the spring of 2001. Local newscasts around the country reported that as many as 10 million Americans suffered from an unrecognized disease. Viewers were urged to watch for the symptoms: restlessness, fatigue, irritability, muscle tension, nausea, diarrhea, and sweating, among others. Many of the segments featured sound bites from Sonja Burkett, a patient who'd finally received treatment after two years trapped at home by the illness, and from Dr. Jack Gorman, an esteemed psychiatrist at Columbia University. Their testimonials were intercut with peaceful images of a woman playing with a bird, and another woman taking pills.

The disease was generalized anxiety disorder (GAD), a condition that, according to the reports, left sufferers paralyzed with irrational fears. Mental-health advocates called it "the forgotten illness." Print periodicals were awash in stories of young women plagued by worries over money and men. "Everything took 10 times more effort for me than it did for anyone else," one woman told the *Chicago Tribune*. "The thing about GAD is that worry can be a full-time job. So if you add that up with what I was doing, which was being a full-time achiever, I was exhausted, constantly exhausted."

Brendan I. Koerner, "Disorders Made to Order: Pharmaceutical Companies Have Come Up with a New Strategy to Market Their Drugs: First Go Out and Find a New Mental Illness, Then Push the Pills to Cure It," *Mother Jones*, July–August 2002. Copyright 2002 Foundation for National Progress. Reproduced by permission.

The timing of the media frenzy was no accident. On April 16, 2001, the U.S. Food and Drug Administration (FDA) had approved the antidepressant Paxil, made by British pharmaceutical giant GlaxoSmithKline, for the treatment of generalized anxiety disorder. But GAD was a little-known ailment; according to a 1989 study, as few as 1.2 percent of the population merited the diagnosis in any given year. If GlaxoSmithKline hoped to capitalize on Paxil's new indication, it would have to raise GAD's profile.

That meant revving up the company's public-relations machinery. The widely featured quotes from Sonja Burkett, and the images of birds and pills, were part of a "video news release" the drugmaker had distributed to TV stations around the country; the footage also included the comments of Dr. Gorman, who has frequently served as a paid consultant to GlaxoSmithKline. On April 16—the date of Paxil's approval—a patient group called Freedom From Fear released a telephone survey according to which "people with GAD spend nearly 40 hours per week, or a 'full-time job,' worrying." The survey mentioned neither GlaxoSmithKline nor Paxil, but the press contact listed was an account executive at Cohn & Wolfe, the drugmaker's P.R. firm.

## Marketing a Disease

GlaxoSmithKline's modus operandi—marketing a disease rather than selling a drug—is typical of the post-Prozac era. "The strategy [companies] use—it's almost mechanized by now," says Dr. Loren Mosher, a San Diego psychiatrist and former official at the National Institute of Mental Health. Typically, a corporate-sponsored "disease awareness" campaign focuses on a mild psychiatric condition with a large pool of potential sufferers. Companies fund studies that prove the drug's efficacy in treating the affliction, a necessary step in obtaining FDA approval for a new use, or "indication." Prominent doctors are enlisted to publicly affirm the malady's ubiquity. Public-relations firms launch campaigns to promote the new disease, using dramatic statistics from corporate-sponsored studies. Finally, patient groups are recruited to serve as the "public face" for the condition, supplying quotes and compelling human stories for the media; many of the groups are heavily subsidized by drugmakers, and some operate directly out of the offices of drug companies' P.R. firms.

The strategy has enabled the pharmaceutical industry to squeeze millions in additional revenue from the blockbuster drugs known as selective serotonin reuptake inhibitors (SSRIS), a family of pharmaceuticals that includes Paxil, Prozac, Zoloft, Celexa, and Luvox. Originally approved solely as antidepressants, the SSRIs are now prescribed for a wide array of heretofore obscure afflictions—GAD, social anxiety disorder, premenstrual dysphoric disorder. The proliferation of diagnoses has contributed to a dramatic rise in antidepressant sales, which increased eightfold between 1990 and 2000. Prozac alone has been used by more than 22 million Americans since it first came to market in 1988.

For pharmaceutical companies, marketing existing drugs for new uses makes perfect sense: A new indication can be obtained in less than 18 months, compared to the eight years it takes to bring a drug from the lab to the pharmacy. Managed-care companies also have been encouraging the use of medication, rather than more costly psychotherapy, to treat problems like anxiety and depression.

---

*If you spend an awful lot of time with pharmaceutical companies, if you talk on their platforms, if you run clinical trials for them, you can't help but be influenced.*

---

But while most health experts agree that SSRIs have revolutionized the treatment of mental illness, a growing number of critics are disturbed by the degree to which corporate-sponsored campaigns have come to define what qualifies as a mental disorder and who needs to be medicated. "You often hear: 'There are 10 million Americans with this, 3 million Americans with that,'" says Barbara Mintzes, an epidemiologist at the University of British Columbia's Centre for Health Services and Policy Research. "If you start adding up all those millions, eventually you'll be hard put to find some Americans who don't have such diagnoses."

## New Uses For Old Drugs

When Paxil hit the market in 1993, the drug's manufacturer, then known as SmithKline Beecham, lagged far behind its competitors. Eli Lilly's Prozac, the first FDA-approved SSRI, had already been around for five years, and Pfizer had beaten SmithKline to the punch with Zoloft's debut in 1992. With only a finite number of depression patients to target, Paxil's sales prospects seemed limited. But SmithKline found a way to set its drug apart from the other SSRIs: It positioned Paxil as an anti-anxiety drug—a latter-day Valium—rather than as a depression treatment.

SmithKline was especially interested in a series of minor entries in the Diagnostic and Statistical Manual of Mental Disorders (DSM), the psychiatric bible. Published by the American Psychiatric Association since the 1950s, the DSM is designed to give doctors and scientists a common set of criteria to describe mental conditions. Entries are often influenced by cultural norms (until 1973, homosexuality was listed as a mental disorder) and political compromise: The manual is written by committees of mental-health professionals who debate, sometimes heatedly, whether to include specific disorders. The entry for GAD, says David Healy, a scholar at the University of Wales College of Medicine and author of the 1998 book *The Antidepressant Era*, was created almost by default: "Floundering somewhat, members of the anxiety disorders subcommittee stumbled on the notion of generalized anxiety disorder," he writes, "and consigned the greater part of the rest of the anxiety disorders to this category."

---

*Because the "Imagine Being Allergic to People" posters did not name a product, they didn't have to mention Paxil's side effects, which can include nausea, decreased appetite, decreased libido, and tremors.*

---

Critics note that the DSM process has no formal safeguards to prevent researchers with drug-company ties from participating in decisions of interest to their sponsors. The committee that recommended the GAD entry in 1980, for example, was headed by Robert L. Spitzer of the New York State Psychiatric Institute, which has been a leading recipient of industry grants to research drug treatments for anxiety disorders. "It's not so much that the industry is there in some Machiavellian way," says Healy. "But if you spend an awful lot of time with pharmaceutical companies, if you talk on their platforms, if you run clinical trials for them, you can't help but be influenced."

## A Rare Form of Shyness in the Spotlight

SmithKline's first forays into the anxiety market involved two fairly well-known illnesses—panic disorder and obsessive-compulsive disorder. Then, in 1998, the company applied for FDA approval to market Paxil for something called social phobia or "social anxiety disorder" (SAD), a debilitating form of shyness the DSM characterized as "extremely rare."

Obtaining such a new indication is a relatively simple affair. The FDA considers a DSM notation sufficient proof that a disease actually exists and, unlike new drugs, existing pharmaceuticals don't require an exhaustive round of clinical studies. To show that a drug works in treating a new disease, the FDA often accepts in-house corporate studies, even when companies refuse to disclose their data or methodologies to other researchers, as is scientific custom.

With FDA approval for Paxil's new use virtually guaranteed, SmithKline turned to the task of promoting the disease itself. To "position social anxiety disorder as a severe condition," as the trade journal PR News put it, the company retained the New York-based public-relations firm Cohn & Wolfe. (Representatives of GlaxoSmithKline and Cohn & Wolfe did not return phone calls.)

By early 1999 the firm had created a slogan, "Imagine Being Allergic to People," and wallpapered bus shelters nationwide with pictures of a dejected-looking man vacantly playing with a teacup. "You blush, sweat, shake—even find it hard to breathe," read the copy. "That's what social anxiety disorder feels like." The posters made no reference to Paxil or SmithKline; instead, they bore the insignia of a group called the Social Anxiety Disorder Coalition and its three nonprofit members, the American Psychiatric Association, the Anxiety Disorders Association of America, and Freedom From Fear.

But the coalition was not a grassroots alliance of patients in search of a cure. It had been cobbled together by SmithKline Beecham, whose P.R. firm, Cohn & Wolfe, handled all media inquiries on behalf of the group. (Today, callers to the coalition's hot line are greeted by a recording that announces simply, "This program has successfully concluded.")

There were numerous good reasons for SmithKline to keep its handiwork discreet. One was the public's mistrust of pharmaceutical companies; another was the FDA's advertising regulations. "If you are carrying out a disease-awareness campaign, legally the company doesn't have to list the product risks," notes Mintzes, the University of British Columbia researcher. Because the "Imagine Being Allergic to People" posters did not name a product, they didn't have to mention Paxil's side effects, which can include nausea, decreased appetite, decreased libido, and tremors.

Cohn & Wolfe's strategy did not end with posters. The firm also created a video news release, a radio news release, and a matte release, a bylined article that smaller newspapers often run unedited. Journalists were given a press packet stating that SAD "affects up to 13.3 percent of the population," or 1 in 8 Americans, and is "the third most common psychiatric disorder in the United States, after depression and alcoholism." By contrast, the Diagnostic and Statistical Manual cites studies showing that between 3 and 13 percent of people may suffer the disease at some point in their lives, but that only 2 percent "experience enough impairment or distress to warrant a diagnosis of social phobia."

Cohn & Wolfe also supplied journalists with eloquent patients, helping to "put a face on the disorder," as account executive Holly White told PR News. P.R. firms often handpick patients to help publicize a disease, offering them media training and sending them on promotional tours. In 1994, for example, drugmakers Upjohn and Solvay funded a traveling art show by Mary Hull, a Californian who suffered from obsessive-compulsive disorder and spoke frequently with journalists about the disorder's toll—as well as her SSRI-aided recovery. Not coincidentally, the companies were awaiting FDA approval to market their SSRI, Luvox, for the treatment of obsessive-compulsive disorder. Among the patients most frequently quoted in stories about social anxiety disorder was a woman named Grace Dailey, who had also appeared in a promotional video produced by Cohn & Wolfe.

Also featured on that video was Jack Gorman, the Columbia University professor who would later make the rounds on Paxil's behalf during the GAD media campaign. Gorman appeared on numerous television shows, including ABC's *Good Morning America*. "It is our hope that patients will now know that they are not alone, that their disease has a name, and it is treatable," he said in a Social Anxiety Disorder Coalition press release.

Dr. Gorman was not a disinterested party in Paxil's promotion. He has served as a paid consultant to at least 13 pharmaceutical firms, including SmithKline Beecham, Eli Lilly, and Pfizer. Another frequent talking head in the SAD campaign, Dr. Murray Stein of the University of California at San Diego, has also served as a SmithKline consultant, and the company funded many of his clinical trials on SAD.

Retaining high-profile academic researchers for promotional purposes is standard practice among drug companies, says Mosher, the former National Institute of Mental Health official. "They are basically paid for going on TV and saying, 'You know, there's this big new problem, and this drug seems to be very helpful.'"

## Industry Praise for Expanding the Anxiety Market

Cohn & Wolfe's full-court press on SAD paid immediate dividends. In the two years preceding Paxil's approval, fewer than 50 stories on social anxiety disorder had appeared in the popular press. In May 1999, the month when the FDA handed down its decision, hundreds of stories about the illness appeared in U.S. publications and television news programs, including the *New York Times, Vogue*, and *Good Morning America*. A few months later, SmithKline launched a series of ads touting Paxil's efficacy in helping SAD sufferers brave dinner parties and public speaking. By the end of last year, Paxil had supplanted Zoloft as the nation's number-two SSRI, and its sales were virtually on par with those of Eli Lilly's Prozac. (Neither Prozac nor Zoloft has an indication for SAD.)

The success of the Cohn & Wolfe campaign didn't escape notice in the industry: Trade journals applauded GlaxoSmithKline for creating "a strong anti-anxiety position" and assuring a bright future for Paxil. Increasing public awareness of SAD and other disorders, the consulting firm Decision Resources predicted last year, would expand the "anxiety market" to at least $3 billion by 2009. In 2000, the New York chapter of the Public Relations Society of America named the Cohn & Wolfe SAD campaign "Best P.R. Program of 1999."

*Current*
**CONTROVERSIES**

# CHAPTER 2

# Are Drugs the Best Way to Treat Mental Illness?

# Chapter Preface

Treating mental illness has evolved significantly since the days when prehistoric societies in Neolithic Europe and South America practiced trepanation, which involved drilling a hole through the skull to release the malignant spirits trapped inside, or the Middle Ages, when mental illness was often diagnosed as witchcraft and hundreds of thousands of "witches" were executed in Europe. Now there are more compassionate, less invasive ways of treating mental illness through the use of drugs that affect the levels of brain chemicals called neurotransmitters.

Drugs for mental illnesses were first introduced in the early 1950s with the anti-psychotic drug chlorpromazine, also known as Thorazine, which treats schizophrenia and other mental disorders. This drug, and other drugs like it that have been developed since, can turn off the voices heard by some people with psychosis and help them to see reality more clearly. Schizophrenia is a complex illness and exactly what causes it is unknown, but it is believed that it may be caused by excessive activity of a neurotransmitter called dopamine in the brain; antipsychotic medications such as Thorazine block dopamine receptors in the brain.

Prozac, introduced in 1987, was ushered in during an era in which many believed that curing mental illnesses such as depression and anxiety disorders was as simple as adjusting a few brain chemicals. Prozac was quickly followed up by other selective serotonin reuptake inhibitors (SSRIs), including Zoloft, Lexapro, and Paxil, which, like Prozac, affect a brain neurotransmitter called serotonin. After several decades on the market enthusiasm for SSRIs is more muted, with many questioning the widespread use of medication that has resulted in only limited gains in public mental health. For example, a 2002 study in *Prevention & Treatment* found that approximately 80% of the response to the six biggest antidepressants of the 1990s was duplicated in control groups who got a placebo.

The controversy is more strident over the use of SSRIs than over antipsychotic drugs, since diseases like severe manic depression (also known as bipolar disorder) and schizophrenia are thought to involve specific brain abnormalities, while the brain processes that result in depression and anxiety are less understood. And almost all experts believe that antipsychotic medications, despite their side effects, improve the quality of life for schizophrenia patients, because they reduce intolerable symptoms that can make life so difficult. But for so-called milder depressive and anxiety disorders, there is tremendous debate about the validity of drug use, especially by children and teens. The long-term risks associated with the use of these drugs are still unknown, and many think these drugs might pose yet-unknown risks for young people, whose brains are still developing.

Despite these caveats, antidepressants aren't going away any time soon, with millions of Americans, including children, taking these drugs and many reporting that SSRIs give them significant relief from their symptoms. In 2005, the Food and Drug Administration (FDA) asked antidepressant drug manufacturers to include a boxed warning label that alerts health care providers to an increased risk of suicidal thinking and behavior in children and teens being treated with these drugs.

# A Combination of Drugs and Therapy Can Help Treat ADHD

*Linda Bren*

*Linda Bren is a staff writer for* FDA Consumer *magazine.*

It seemed that the harder he tried, the worse things got for Robert Jergen. As a child, he was always being scolded by his parents and teachers. As an adult, his bosses reprimanded him for missed deadlines and his attitude problem. He got fired from jobs, drank heavily, and lost his fiancé.

But Jergen wasn't a slouch, a drunk, or intentionally obnoxious. He had a condition called attention-deficit hyperactivity disorder (ADHD).

"I wanted to be a good kid, but I frequently did things without thinking or without even realizing that I did them," says Jergen. Problems with concentration continued to plague him as an adult. In collage, Jergen would stay up all night trying to finish his schoolwork. "I could not focus my attention on the page long enough to read a paragraph. My thoughts raced round and round in my head. It's like my mind was a pinball machine with five or six balls smashing into each other."

ADHD is the most commonly diagnosed mental health disorder in children, according to the American Psychiatric Association. It's often diagnosed once a child hits preschool and is disruptive in class—unable to sit still, talking incessantly, and having emotional outbursts. While some children see their symptoms fade as they get older, others carry them into adolescence and adulthood.

Although there is no cure for ADHD, medications [a]nd behavioral therapy can help treat the symptoms. The Food and Drug Administration has approved two drugs for adults with ADHD, and more have been approved for use in children. But the decision to take medication should be considered carefully and discussed with a health professional, says Paul Andreason, M.D., a drug reviewer in the FDA's Division of Neuropharmacological Drug Products. Some drugs used to treat ADHD can be dangerous for adults with certain medical conditions. They also have the potential for addiction and abuse. Adults taking medications should be closely monitored by a physician. Children, too, who take drugs for ADHD need regular medical checkups.

## Three Types of ADHD

Everyone has trouble sitting still sometimes, or managing time, or completing a task. But the behavior of people with ADHD goes beyond occasional fidgeting, disorganization, and procrastination. For them, performing tasks can be so hard that it interferes with their ability to function at work, at home, at school, and socially.

A diagnostic manual compiled by the American Psychiatric Association identifies three types of ADHD: inattentive, hyperactive-impulsive, and combined.

A person with inattentive ADHD, previously known as attention-deficit disorder (ADD), has trouble focusing on activities, organizing and finishing tasks, and following instructions.

Children with hyperactive-impulsive ADHD are in constant motion, dashing around touching everything in sight, and jumping on and off furniture. They often blurt out inappropriate comments, don't wait their turn, show excessively intense emotions, or hit others when upset. Hyperactive and impulsive adults feel restless, are constantly "on the go," and try to do multiple tasks at once. They are often perceived as not thinking before they act or speak.

Individuals with the combined form of ADHD show symptoms of both inattention and hyperactivity-impulsivity.

## Who Has It?

The National Institute of Mental Health (NIMH) estimates that between 3 percent and 5 percent of children in the United States have ADHD. This means that in a classroom of 25 to 30 children, it is likely that at least one will have ADHD. Three times as many boys are diagnosed with ADHD, but "girls are getting diagnosed more and more," says Nora Galil, M.D., a psychiatrist in private practice in Washington, D.C. The symptoms may be easier to spot in boys, she says, who may be seen slipping from their chairs and tossing things across the room. "You can often identify it in a short period of time because they are so disruptive. Girls may be the ones who daydream and are not disruptive, so it's not picked up nearly as much."

The number of adults with ADHD is unknown, and medical experts continue to debate whether children can expect to outgrow the symptoms of ADHD by the time they reach adulthood.

Some studies have shown a significant decline in ADHD symptoms as a person ages. Others estimate that between 30 percent and 70 percent of children with ADHD will continue to have symptoms into adulthood.

"In adults, it's a much more elaborate disorder than in children," says Russell Barkley, Ph.D., a psychiatry professor at the Medical University of South Carolina. "It's more than paying attention and controlling impulses. The problem is developing self-regulation." This self-control affects an adult's ability not just to do tasks, but to determine when they need to be done, says Barkley. "You don't expect 4- or 5-year-olds to have a sense of time and organization, but adults need goal-directed behavior—they need help in planning for the future and remembering things that have to get done."

## The Consequences of ADHD

Whether in a child or an adult, ADHD can have serious consequences. Some studies show that children with ADHD have more emergency room visits than their non-ADHD peers. Adolescents with ADHD are more likely to engage in risky behavior, leading to substance abuse, sexually transmitted diseases, and teen pregnancy.

Adolescents and young adults are more likely to drop out of school and less likely to enter and graduate from college, according to some studies. And adults with ADHD are more likely to suffer from depression and anxiety, be fired from jobs, and get divorced than non-ADHD adults.

Teens and adults with ADHD have 2 to 3 times more auto accidents and twice the number of severe accidents resulting in vehicle damage and bodily injury as those without ADHD, according to studies done by Barkley and others. "They have coordination deficits, less skill in maneuvering vehicles in traffic, slower reaction time, and inattention," says Barkley.

---

*Differences exist between the brains of children with and without ADHD.*

---

People with ADHD often have "a huge issue of self-esteem," says Galil. "They may have been underachievers and told 'you're so smart, why can't you do this? You're not trying hard enough.'"

Jergen says he always tried very hard, but he couldn't focus his mind on the task at hand. He likens it to having a song or jingle in your head for days at a time, but "add three or four or five more thoughts to the mix and amplify them. Spin them round and round and round in your head and make them go faster and faster and faster until they become like an all-consuming obsession. Everything centers on those thoughts. You can't focus on anything else. You can't escape them."

## Not a Discipline Problem

ADHD was once looked upon as a discipline and behavioral problem resulting from bad parenting. Some suggested it was caused by high sugar intake, food additives, excessive TV viewing, and family problems. But none of these explanations is supported by scientific evidence.

Most scientists agree that it's a biologically based disorder of the nervous system. Brain imaging research using a technique called magnetic resonance imaging (MRI) has shown that differences exist between the brains of children with and without ADHD, but the exact mechanism of brain function causing the symptoms of ADHD is unknown. Scientists caution that MRIs used in studies are research tools and cannot be used to diagnose ADHD in a specific person.

Recently published research suggests that ADHD tends to run in families. In these studies, children with ADHD have, on average, at least one close relative with ADHD. Over the years, other theories have suggested that exposure to lead in the environment, premature birth, birth trauma, and brain injury may lead to the development of ADHD. Some studies have shown a possible correlation between the use of cigarettes and alcohol during pregnancy and the risk for giving birth to a child with ADHD. For this and many other health reasons, the NIMH recommends that women who are pregnant refrain from both cigarette and alcohol use.

## Diagnosing ADHD

There is no single test to determine if a person has ADHD. A specialist makes the diagnosis by comparing a person's pattern of behavior against a set of criteria established by the American Psychiatric Association.

"Sometimes teachers may identify a child as potentially having ADHD," says Galil. "Parents will not always know because they organize and structure and manage so much of the child's life, it masks what's going on."

Although teachers and parents may recognize some symptoms, it's important to get a diagnosis from a health professional, ideally one with training in ADHD and mental disorders, says the NIMH. This may be a psychiatrist, psychologist, behavioral neurologist, or a developmental or behavioral pediatrician. More than one health professional may be consulted to diagnose and treat ADHD, since medical and psychological tests, medication, and counseling may be involved.

"Many health professionals believe that ADHD is over-diagnosed," says Andreason, and doctors need to consider the complete history of patients before diagnosing them.

"It's a hard diagnosis to tease out, and we need to spend some time asking questions about all areas of their life," adds Edmund Higgins, M.D., clinical assistant professor of family medicine and psychiatry at the Medical University of South Carolina and a psychiatrist in private practice.

Some adults may discover they have ADHD only after their children are diagnosed with the disorder. That's how Toni Wood found out she had it.

Wood, of Chesapeake, Va., was a hyperactive child, always getting into trouble at school and always in the principal's office, she says. "If I was quiet, I was sick." Throughout her school years, she had a hard time processing information and asked a lot of questions in class. "It really frustrated me, and everybody was looking at me and rolling their eyes. I knew I wasn't stupid, but I was always behind."

---

*Stimulants can improve alertness and attention without making the hyperactivity worse.*

---

Wood persevered, graduating from high school, serving in the U.S. Coast Guard, and going to college. Civilian life was daunting for her after the structured military environment where "they told you what to wear and what to do," says Wood. She graduated from college, but continued to have difficulty with daily [a]ctivities—paying bills and completing tasks, especially in the evening when she was most fidgety and inattentive. "I thought I was going crazy," she says.

At age 38, Wood found out that she wasn't crazy. After both her sons were diagnosed with ADHD, Wood's doctor diagnosed her with the condition, too. She felt a weight being lifted off her shoulders, she says. "I'm not using ADHD as an excuse; it's an explanation. Now I understand why."

## Treatments for ADHD

A number of FDA-approved medications are available to help treat the symptoms of ADHD. Some people have better results from one drug, some from another. "But treatments need to involve a behavior modification program," says Andreason. "Medicine is only an adjunct to behavior modification."

Children with ADHD may require emotional counseling and behavioral management involving parents, teachers, and health professionals. Adults with ADHD may benefit from counseling, vocational guidance, and professional coaching done by specialists who help individuals develop coping skills and methods for organization and time management.

---

*Children who take stimulants may grow and gain weight more slowly and growth should be monitored by their pediatricians.*

---

Jergen has developed his own coping strategies, and daily exercise is an important one. "When my mind is in a fog, I get on the treadmill and break a sweat, the fog parts, and I can concentrate," he says. He's also set up his office environment with special lighting and soft music to help him relax and concentrate.

People with ADHD may be hyperactive, but, surprisingly, they are often prescribed a stimulant to help treat the symptoms. Stimulants can improve alertness and attention without making the hyperactivity worse.

FDA-approved stimulants for children ages 6 and older include products containing various forms of methylphenidate, amphetamine, and methamphetamine.

In August 2004, the extended-release form of the stimulant Adderall (Adderall XR), previously approved to treat children with ADHD, was also approved to treat adults with ADHD. An extended-release form of a drug works in the body over a longer time than an immediate-release form, allowing the medication to be taken less frequently.

Adderall or other stimulants should not be taken by people with certain conditions, including hyperthyroidism, glaucoma, moderate-to-severe hypertension, other heart-related conditions, or a history of drug abuse. Some common side effects of stimulants are insomnia, decreased appetite, and increased anxiety or irritability. Children who take stimulants may grow and gain weight more slowly, and growth should be monitored by their pediatricians.

Because stimulant medicines have a high potential for abuse, the U.S. Drug Enforcement Administration has placed stringent controls on them. For example, the DEA requires special licenses to manufacture, distribute, and prescribe these controlled substances, and prescription refills aren't allowed.

One other drug, Strattera (atomoxetine), is FDA-approved for use in adults with ADHD as well as in adolescents and children ages 6 and older. Strattera is not classified as a stimulant and does not seem to have a potential for abuse. It is not classified as a controlled substance, so it can be prescribed with refills. Strattera increases the levels of the neurotransmitter norepinephrine in the brain, whereas the stimulants work primarily on the neurotransmitter dopamine. Strattera may take three or four weeks for its full effectiveness to kick in; stimulants can have a nearly immediate effect in some patients.

Strattera causes an increase in heart rate and blood pressure and should be used with caution in people with hypertension or heart-related conditions. In clinical studies, the most common side effects of Strattera in adults were dry mouth, headache, insomnia, nausea, decreased appetite, and constipation. In children and adolescents, common side effects were stomachache, headache, and decreased appetite. Like stimulants, Strattera may slow weight gain and growth in children, and these measures should be monitored by a pediatrician.

## Treatment Decisions

Galil, who treats both children and adults with ADHD, says she doesn't use medications as frequently in adults. Parents bring children to her because they're not doing well at school or their behavior is disruptive, she says, but adults who haven't been diagnosed as children often "have found ways to cope without medication for years." Sometimes, she'll prescribe a stimulant as needed for specific tasks, such as for an events planner who was "marvelous at events with a headset on and 4,000 people around her, putting out a fire a minute," but didn't do well sitting back at the home office doing paperwork. So she'd take medication on a day that she needed to spend time on paperwork.

"With children, it's different," says Galil. "They often benefit from medication seven days a week. Adults, by and large, don't want to be on medication all the time." But with diagnosis and treatment, "some who never finished college or graduate school now have the tools to go back and finish."

Wood is one of these. Since she's been on medication, she went back to college and earned a second degree. "I saw such a difference," she says. "College was so much easier" and so were routine household tasks, like paying bills. Wood is now an ADHD coach, helping other people cope with the disorder.

Once he was diagnosed with ADHD at age 24, Jergen said it took about two years of trying different medications and dosages to find out what worked best for him. Like Wood, he found that tasks became easier for him. He got his doctorate in special education, published five books in two years, and became an associate professor at the University of Wisconsin-Oshkosh. "I have a lot of energy and I don't sleep a lot," says Jergen, who recounts his experiences with ADHD in his book, *The Little Monster: Growing Up With ADHD.* Jergen urges parents of children with ADHD to help them use the energy to be productive instead of making them slow down.

After 10 years of taking various stimulants, antidepressants, and mood stabilizers, Jergen went off medications in 2002 because of their sexual side effects and the development of a vocal tic that caused him to make involuntary noises. He continues teaching and writing, recently got married, and says, "My life is just fantastic."

"I'm still hyperactive, impulsive, and inattentive," adds Jergen. "If I were an air traffic controller, planes would be crashing." But Jergen, known as a dynamic speaker, says he's in his element in front of a class.

## Drug Risks and Precautions

Public health officials are concerned that stimulants may be inappropriately prescribed for some adults with ADHD. "Stimulants do work, but we know that they increase blood pressure and pulse rate," says Andreason, which could lead to strokes and heart attacks. "These drugs are very strongly labeled for their risk to the cardiovascular system," he adds.

"Patients with hypertension shouldn't be getting stimulants," says Kate Gelperin, M.D., a medical officer in the FDA's Office of Drug Safety. "If your blood pressure is on the high side, these drugs are not for you." About one-third of U.S. adults have high blood pressure, according to a study published in the October 2004 issue of *Hypertension*, a journal of the American Heart Association.

Raymond Woosley, M.D., Ph.D., a clinical pharmacologist and vice president for health sciences at the University of Arizona, says, "There are a lot of people who don't know they have hypertension or heart disease. In many people, the first symptom of heart disease is sudden death." Woosley advises adults with ADHD who are prescribed stimulants to "make sure their doctor is fully informed of their total medical condition and get a complete medical workup to make sure they're not at risk."

Even those without hypertension who take stimulants may be at risk, says Gelperin. "It's not known whether adults who take stimulants over long periods of time may have an increased risk of sudden death, stroke, or heart attack," she says, "although we do know that people who take an overdose of stimulants experience these adverse effects."

---

*Some people will like the effects of the stimulants—either performance enhancement or the euphoria—and will want to be diagnosed as having ADHD.*

---

Woosley also recommends that parents get their children checked by a qualified pediatrician before giving them stimulants for ADHD. Parents should not insist on a stimulant for their child based on the positive experience of a friend's child who is taking the stimulant or because a teacher suggests it, he says. A child should be examined by a doctor and diagnosed with ADHD before being placed on a stimulant. "A stimulant given to a child with ADHD can help to normalize them," he says, "but if given to someone who doesn't have the right diagnosis, it can make them worse." Once prescribed a stimulant, a child's blood pressure and heart rate should be monitored closely until the dosage is stabilized, and then yearly, says Woosley, since the way the body responds to medication is highly variable and may change over time.

Research has shown that people with ADHD who take stimulants in the form and dosage prescribed do not appear to be at as great a risk for addiction as previously feared. However, when stimulants are abused, the consequences can be extremely dangerous—even deadly. According to the National Institute on Drug Abuse, taking high doses of a stimulant can cause an irregular heartbeat, dangerously high body temperatures, and heart failure or lethal seizures.

"The FDA has received many reports over the years describing serious adverse effects, including death, associated with stimulant abuse or overdose," says Gelperin.

"Some people will like the effects of the stimulant—either performance enhancement or the euphoria—and will want to be diagnosed as having ADHD," says Higgins. "Where I get concerned is when college students or even professionals come to me and say, 'I have trouble with attention.' Everyone has trouble with attention at some point—particularly with boring tasks." We need to separate patients with some symptoms of ADHD from those who have a genuine disorder, he says.

Higgins is also troubled by parents who take their child's stimulant or someone else's and claim they feel better. "Stimulants are basically 'speed,'" he says, "and most people will be more productive with them. That doesn't mean they have a disorder."

Higgins says that, in his practice, he reserves stimulants for people who have severe impairment, for whom Strattera doesn't work, and who are not at risk for substance abuse.

# Antidepressants Can Help Treat Childhood Depression

## National Institute of Mental Health

*The National Institute of Mental Health (NIMH) is part of the federal government of the United States and the largest research organization in the world specializing in mental illness.*

Depression is a serious disorder that can cause significant problems in mood, thinking, and behavior at home, in school, and with peers. It is estimated that major depressive disorder (MDD) affects about 5 percent of adolescents, who have more frequent suicidal thinking and behavior and greater likelihood of substance abuse than youth in general.

Research has shown that, as in adults, depression in children and adolescents can be treated. In particular, antidepressant medications—called selective serotonin reuptake inhibitors (SSRIs) because they specifically target the neurotransmitter serotonin—have been shown to be of benefit to children and adolescents with major depressive disorder. Certain types of psychological therapies have also been shown to be beneficial. In those with moderate to severe depression they are especially useful when combined with medication. Our knowledge of antidepressant treatments in youth, though growing substantially, remains limited when compared with what we know about treatment of depression in adults.

Recently, concerns have been raised that the use of antidepressant medications themselves may induce suicidal behavior in youths. In fact, following a thorough and comprehensive review of all the available published and unpublished controlled clinical trials of antidepressants in children and adolescents, the FDA has warned the public about an increased risk

National Institute of Mental Health, "Antidepressant Medications for Children and Adolescents: Information For Parents and Caregivers," www.nimh.nih.gov, February 8, 2005. Reproduced by permission.

of suicidal thoughts or behavior ("suicidality") in children and adolescents treated with SSRI antidepressant medications.

Studies show that there are substantial benefits from medication treatment for adolescents with moderate and severe depression, including many with suicidal ideation. [A review of numerous studies on children and antidepressants found that] no completed suicides occurred among nearly 2,200 children treated with SSRI medications; however, the rate of suicidal thinking or behavior, including actual suicidal attempts, was 4 percent for those on SSRI medications, twice the rate of those on inert placebo pills (2 percent).

The FDA adopted a "black box" label warning that antidepressants were found to increase the risk of suicidal thinking and behavior in children and adolescents with major depressive disorder. A black-box warning is the most serious type of warning in prescription drug labeling.

The warning also emphasizes that children and adolescents started on SSRI medications should be closely monitored for any worsening in depression, emergence of suicidal thinking or behavior, and in general for any unusual changes in behavior—such as sleeplessness, agitation, withdrawal from normal social situations. This monitoring is especially important during the first four weeks of treatment. SSRI medications usually have few side effects in children and adolescents, but for unknown reasons, can trigger agitation and abnormal behavior in certain individuals.

## What Do We Know About Antidepressant Medications?

SSRI medications are considered an improvement over older antidepressant medications because they have fewer side effects and are safer if taken in an overdose (which is an issue for patients at risk for suicide). They have been extensively tested in adult populations and have been proven to be safe and effective for adults.

Use of SSRI medications has risen dramatically in the past several years in children and adolescents age 10–19. Some studies show that this increase has coincided with a significant decrease in suicide rates in this age group, but it is not known if SSRI medications are directly responsible for this improvement.

Fluoxetine (also known as Prozac) is the only medication approved by the FDA for use to treat depression in children age 8 and older. The other SSRI medications, such as sertraline, citalopram, and paroxetine, and the SSRI-related antidepressant venlafaxine, have not been approved for treatment of depression in children or adolescents, though they have been prescribed to children by physicians in "off-label use"—a use other than the FDA approved use. In June 2003, the FDA recommended that paroxetine not be used in children and adolescents for the treatment of major depressive disorder.

---

*It is extremely difficult to determine whether SSRI medications do or do not increase the risk of completed suicide, especially since depression itself increases the risk of suicide and because completed suicide is a rare event.*

---

Fluoxetine has been shown to be helpful for treating childhood depression in three different clinical trials—two supported by NIMH and the other supported by the manufacturer of the drug. The trials found that fluoxetine by itself, and even more so when combined with cognitive behavioral therapy, reduced depression for many children better than an inert placebo pill. However, fluoxetine failed to improve depression in at least one third of patients. Also, about one in 10 children experienced adverse side effects such as agitation and mania.

In the recently completed Treatment for Adolescents with Depression Study (TADS) funded by NIMH, suicidal thinking generally decreased during treatment with fluoxetine, but 15 of the 216 youths on fluoxetine (6.94 percent) had a suicide-related event, such as a suicidal attempt or threats, as compared with 9 of the 223 on the inert placebo pill (4.04 percent).

Fluoxetine leads to significant improvement of depression overall. The drug, however, may increase the risk for suicidal behaviors *in a small subset of adolescents.* As with all medical decisions, doctors and families have to weigh risks and benefits of treatment for each individual patient.

## What Remains Unknown

Currently, there is no way of telling who may be sensitive to an SSRI's positive or adverse effects. Results thus far are based on populations—some individuals may show marked improvement, some may see no change, and some may be vulnerable to adverse effects. The response to medication of an individual patient cannot be predicted with certainty from the kind of studies that have been done so far.

It is extremely difficult to determine whether SSRI medications do or do not increase the risk of completed suicide, especially since depression itself increases the risk for suicide and because completed suicide is a rare event. Controlled trials typically include only hundreds of patients, not the thousands needed to detect effects for rare events. In addition, controlled trials typically exclude patients considered at high risk for suicide, such as those with a history of suicide attempts.

## What Should You Do for a Child with Depression?

Major depression in children and adolescents is a serious condition that should be adequately treated, which includes careful follow-up and monitoring.

Each child should be carefully and thoroughly evaluated by a physician to determine if medication is appropriate.

Those who are prescribed an SSRI medication should receive ongoing medical monitoring, with particular care paid in the first four weeks of taking the drug.

Psychotherapy is often used as an initial treatment for milder forms of depression. Many times, psychotherapy accompanied by an early follow-up appointment may help to establish the persistence of depression before a decision is made to try antidepressant medications. Psychotherapies include "cognitive behavioral therapy" and "interpersonal therapy." For moderate to severe forms of depression, especially if persistent, the current evidence supports the use of fluoxetine alone or in combination with cognitive-behavioral therapy (CBT).

Should suicidal thinking or behavior, nervousness, agitation, irritability, mood instability, or sleeplessness emerge or worsen during treatment with SSRI medications, parents should obtain a prompt evaluation by a clinician with expertise in these medications.

Children already on any of the SSRI medications should remain on the drug if it has been helpful but they should also be carefully monitored by a physician for evidence of side effects. Once started, treatment with these medications should not be abruptly stopped, because of potential side effects. Families should not discontinue treatment without consulting with their physician.

All treatments can be associated with side effects. A careful weighing of risks and benefits, with appropriate follow-up to help reduce risks, is the best that can be currently recommended.

# Drug Treatment for Mental Illness May Alter Children's Brains

*Alison Motluk*

*Alison Motluk is* New Scientist's *Toronto correspondent.*

ONE day he was a happy, well-adjusted 7-year-old, then suddenly, it seemed, he couldn't stop washing his hands. Nine or ten scrubbings and he still couldn't shake the feeling of being dirty. Then there were his visits to the library. As he left, he was always convinced he'd taken something without checking it out, though he couldn't think what. It was just a nagging feeling that wouldn't go away. "Jason" had somehow developed obsessive compulsive disorder (OCD).

Childhood infections, broken bones, schoolyard bullies—parents are more than ready for these. But a diagnosis of mental illness can catch even the most vigilant parents off guard. We know so little about what causes these illnesses, and still less about how to treat them. Yet more than one in three of our children will struggle with the likes of anxiety or depression, obsessive compulsive thoughts or attention deficit hyperactivity disorder (ADHD) during their childhood.

The trend these days is to treat mental illness in children, as in adults, with drugs. In the US, sales of psychotropic medicines are growing faster than those of any other type of childhood drug. There is some debate about why this is happening—whether the incidence of disease is growing, detection is improving, or diagnostic categories are changing. Many people nurture a gut feeling that lots of children are being medicated unnecessarily. Whatever the cause, their numbers are growing—and the children affected are getting younger. Among pre-schoolers, treatment rates have more than doubled in the past two decades.

## Too Many Mysteries Surround Childhood Drug Treatment for Mental Illness

But how much do we know about how these drugs affect youngsters? "The truth is, it hasn't been studied much," says James Leckman, a child psychiatrist at Yale University. Can drugs designed for and tested in adults even be expected to work in children? Their bodies are different and their brains are still developing. Some studies suggest that administering these drugs to children could alter the structure and chemistry of their brains—at best providing a cure, but at worst trading a mild mental illness for a more serious one.

Many drugs used to treat children with psychiatric problems have only recently begun to be evaluated for their age group. The exceptions are stimulants such as Ritalin, used to treat ADHD, several of which have been approved for children. Most antidepressants, antipsychotics and mood stabilisers are prescribed for children "off label", on the strength of a reasonable performance in adults. In 1997, the US Food and Drug Administration (FDA) was given the power to request that drug companies do clinical trials specifically in children in exchange for six extra months of patent protection.

The clinical trials that have been carried out in minors aren't always reassuring. For instance, in studies of selective serotonin reuptake inhibitors, or SSRIs—used to treat depression, anxiety, OCD and anorexia nervosa—few show that the drug worked better in children with depression than a placebo. A paper in the *British Medical Journal* this April reviewed six studies of SSRIs in children, and concluded that for depression, efficacy was "exaggerated", adverse effects "downplayed" and added benefit over placebo was "of doubtful clinical significance". "The evidence that they work is skimpy," agrees Normand Carrey, a child psychiatrist at Dalhousie University in Halifax, Canada.

---

*Developing brains are profoundly different from the mature brains these drugs were designed for.*

---

And to make things worse, these studies also reveal that children are prone to more severe side effects. Agitation, irritability and disinhibition, which occasionally affect adults, are much more likely to show up in younger SSRI users. In clinical trials, about one in four under-18s taking SSRIs had serious behavioural reactions, such as uncontrollable rages or violent impulses like jumping out of a window, says Jane Garland of the University of British Columbia in Vancouver. In a study on paroxetine (known as Paxil in the US and Seroxat in the UK) in adolescents, she says, 7.5 per cent of the patients taking the drug had to be treated in hospital for adverse effects. None taking a placebo did. Ritalin also has more side effects in young people, says Carrey. The younger the patient, the more severe they are.

Today only Prozac is approved in the US for use in children with depression, although not everyone believes it should be. The drug did get a pat on the back this June, when a large US government-funded study showed it to be considerably more effective than either placebo or talk therapy. Still, the FDA intends to hold public meetings on the use of all SSRIs in children. The decision follows publication of a series of papers this spring, including the *British Medical Journal* study, which revealed that evidence showing lack of effectiveness and increased agitation and suicidal tendencies was glossed over in both the published and unpublished work. In fact, the attorney-general of New York state is suing GlaxoSmithKline, the maker of Paxil, for alleged fraud in not making public all five studies it carried out on the drug, and instead highlighting only the most favourable one.

## Children's Brains Are Different

It comes as no surprise to researchers in the field when modern psychoactive drugs act differently in children. Making adult drugs right for younger patients involves more than just adjusting for lower weight—their bodies have less fat, more water, a higher metabolism and raging hormones. What's more, developing brains are profoundly different from the mature brains these drugs were designed for, says Garland.

---

*Throughout development, receptors all over the brain are blinking on and off. Simply put, the childhood brain is a moving target.*

---

A child's central nervous system has more of almost everything: neurons, connections, neurotransmitters and growth factors. In adults, low levels of the neurotransmitter serotonin have been linked to low moods, and SSRIs work by blocking the absorption of serotonin in the brain and, some think, by stimulating the growth of new neurons. But this raises some interesting questions. Children are already undergoing neurogenesis, Carrey points out. While extra neurons may be a good thing for a depressed adult, they may have completely different implications for a depressed child.

Serotonin levels also appear to differ with age: children's brains synthesise much more than adults'. Diane Chugani at Wayne State University in Detroit found that under-fives produced twice as much serotonin as adults. Thereafter, levels declined slowly toward puberty. Many neurotransmitters, including dopamine, the brain chemical affected by Ritalin, and GABA, which is implicated in anxiety disorders, also show huge variations across the early years. Most are higher early on and come down with age, but the picture is complicated, says Chugani.

Throughout development, receptors all over the brain are blinking on and off. Simply put, the childhood brain is a moving target. "Drugs of many different classes would be expected to behave differently in children," says Chugani, "not only because of levels of neurotransmitters, but also because receptors are different and how they're distributed may be different." That's why it's so important that drugs be studied directly in children, she says, and not extrapolated from adult findings.

Carrey agrees. He was intrigued by a handful of studies that suggested that the same mental disorders were somehow different in children than in adults. One study was of children and adults with OCD; another investigated people who were overly aggressive. The findings in both suggested that young people with these disorders may have overactive serotonin systems—exactly the opposite to what is found in adults. The obvious question was whether antidepressants would work differently in adults and children.

Carrey and his colleagues started to address the question in studies of old and young rats. They found that antidepressants didn't seem to alter a hormonal response controlled by the serotonin system in younger animals the way they did in older ones. He thinks this may be because younger animals' brains are already awash with serotonin, so the SSRI simply couldn't boost serotonin's effect any further. What's more, the serotonin systems in their brains are probably too immature to respond properly to antidepressants.

## Drugs Can Alter a Child's Brain Chemistry and Anatomy

Carrey is also comparing Ritalin in the young and old. Some years ago, questions were raised about whether the drug, which is pharmacologically very similar to cocaine, might predispose children to serious drug abuse. The idea was that years of Ritalin use might "prime" a child's brain to trigger strong cravings for cocaine even after just one exposure to it. In a landmark paper, Nora Volkow, then at Brookhaven National Laboratory in New York state, showed that injected Ritalin acted almost identically to cocaine in adults. "Nobody's bothered to look at how Ritalin affects the developing brain," notes Carrey.

Three studies published together in the journal *Biological Psychiatry* last December tackled that question in animal models. All three found effects that persisted into adulthood. Cindy Brandon and her team at the Chicago Medical School found that taking Ritalin during adolescence made a rat more likely to self-administer cocaine, suggesting they craved rewards more and might be more likely to become addicts later. Underpinning their behaviour were long-lasting neuronal changes. But both William Carlezon at Harvard Medical School and Carlos Bolanos at the University of Texas Southwestern Medical Center in Dallas found the opposite when the drug was given earlier, in the rat equivalent of childhood: then adult rats were less likely to seek rewards. It would be foolish to extrapolate too far, but this work hints that if you're going to treat children with stimulants, better do it in childhood rather than adolescence.

These studies and others raise the disturbing question of whether giving such drugs in childhood will trigger permanent changes in the brain. Neurotransmitters act as developmental signals in the young brain along with their everyday job of trading nerve impulses. Serotonin, for instance, modulates events like cell division, differentiation and migration, and construction of new nerve connections. In animals, raising or lowering the levels of serotonin can disrupt these processes, with lifelong effect. Says Carrey: "I think right now my findings indicate that these are drugs that modify the nervous system, and we have to be cautious."

There are hints that this is true for human patients too. At Wayne State University in Detroit, David Rosenberg has found structural and chemical changes in the brains of young people who are taking psychotropic drugs. He studied children with OCD who were treated off-label with paroxetine and found shrinkage in the thalamus, the brain's main sensory filter.

The good news is that their thalamuses were overly large to begin with, which may have been part of the problem. The drug reduced them to a more normal size. But it shows why a proper diagnosis is so important. Schizophrenia, for instance, is associated with an abnormally small thalamus—something no doctor would want to induce. "It underscores why we have to be careful about using medications," says Rosenberg. "This is altering brain chemistry and anatomy."

Rosenberg's team is studying how persistent these changes are. "The question we're looking into is: what happens to the chemistry and structure when you stop?" They also want to find markers for who might benefit most from drug therapy. "What was exciting about this finding was that the bigger the size of the thalamus [beforehand], the more likely the person was to respond."

---

*There is a flipside to all of this: drugs taken early in life might tackle the source of the disease.*

---

Another vexing question is whether medicating a young brain could in fact turn one mental illness into another. So far, there is more anecdote than evidence on this front, but Carlezon's work in rats, for instance, indicates that Ritalin treatment before adolescence could spell an adulthood of depression. Rats on Ritalin exhibited what he called "learned helplessness" in adulthood—under stress, they gave up on tasks rather quickly, something he believes parallels human depression. He thinks stimulants may affect nerve connections made during development.

And Jane Costello at Duke University in Durham, North Carolina, found that whether treated or not, a child who has had a brush with one psychiatric disorder will be much more likely to have another. In a paper in press, Leckman and Andres Martin from Yale show that drugs may further increase the chance of such "conversion events". Examining four years of insurance records for 100,000 claimants, they found that young people treated with antidepressants—tricyclics and SSRIs—were more likely to be later diagnosed with bipolar disorder than people whose depression wasn't treated with drugs. It looks as if these drugs are a contributing factor, Leckman says. Interestingly, he notes that these medications are increasingly used in younger and younger groups. "It happens to correspond to a time when bipolar disorder is on the rise," he says.

## The Flipside: The Right Drugs at the Right Time Can Help

Of course, illnesses themselves might also have long-lasting detrimental effects on the brain. "Having gone through major depression," says Leckman, "a person may not be the same." And as with the shrinking thalamus in Rosenberg's OCD patients, there is a flipside to all this: drugs taken early in life might tackle the source of the disease.

Chugani, for one, believes childhood is both a time of vulnerability and of opportunity. Her main clinical work is with autism. Her studies of serotonin synthesis have revealed that young autistic children have markedly lower levels in their brains than their non-autistic counterparts. Work in rats and mice has shown that the developing brain needs just the right amount of serotonin to get the thalamus to connect properly to the cortex; one problem in autism may be that a lack of serotonin prevents axons from making that connection. "Too much or too little and they don't form properly," says Chugani. She thinks that augmenting serotonin function in the brains of autistic children could have lifelong implications—permanently reversing some of the deficits of the disease.

She has reason to be hopeful. Evidence from the lab of Rene Hen at Columbia University in New York suggests there are certain windows of opportunity for neurotransmitters like serotonin to work their magic. Hen and his team have been working with mice genetically altered so that specific serotonin receptors can be turned on and off. For example, when one of the receptors for serotonin, the 1A receptor, is not functioning, a mouse will be very anxious. If you keep the 1A receptor switched off for the first three weeks of life, then turn it on for the rest, the mouse will still be anxious. But if you switch it on for the first three weeks, then switch it off ever after, the animal will never display this anxiety. Clearly, a mouse's temperament is at least partly set up during those first critical three weeks.

The more we know about what happens in these critical windows, the more we can imagine such permanent interventions. But we're not there yet; we're not even close. Where we are is surrounded by uncomfortable alternatives.

Intensive forms of talk therapy, while sometimes as good as or even better than medication, can be expensive and hard to come by. We need more professionals, and more money to fund them. Basic science has to study young animals and develop drugs specific to children's needs. Leaving a child to the ravages of mental illness is scarcely an option. "Depression," Rosenberg says, "is a lethal illness." Up to 20 percent of depressed youngsters commit suicide. Kids with psychiatric problems of all kinds face a potentially bleak future if they fail to receive treatment. They have more troubles in school, in holding down jobs, in relationships. One way or another, mental illness costs.

# Antidepressants Can Increase Suicide Risk

## David Stipp

*David Stipp covers science and medicine for* Fortune Magazine.

Can Prozac make you want to die? The idea seems strange, given that the drug and similar antidepressants are supposed to do just the opposite. Yet that is what Kimberly Witczak believes happened to her husband. . . . Tim "Woody" Witczak killed himself at age 37, soon after going on Pfizer's Zoloft—the top-selling member of Prozac's class of drugs, known as selective serotonin reuptake inhibitors, or SSRIs. Her husband was an upbeat, happy man, says Kim Witczak. Shortly before his death he had been named vice president of sales at a startup that sold energy-efficient lighting. When anxiety about the new job caused insomnia, he was prescribed Zoloft. He began suffering from nightmares, profound agitation, and eerie sensory experiences after a couple of weeks on the medicine—at one point, she says, he said he felt as if his head were detached from his body. Then he seemed to calm down. But about five weeks after his first dose, he hanged himself from the rafters in their garage when Kim was out of town. He left no suicide note.

"Woody's death was the most out-of-the-blue, out-of-character death," she told *Fortune* recently. "He had no history of mental illness." Kim Witczak, who lives in Minneapolis, has sued Pfizer, alleging that Zoloft induced the suicide and that the company failed to warn about the drug's potential to cause perilous side effects. Pfizer declined to comment while the case is in litigation, but a spokesman asserted that there is "no scientifically based" evidence to suggest Zoloft can induce violent acts. It's not the first time SSRI makers have faced complaints related to suicide or other forms of violence. They have fended off or quietly settled scores of such suits over the years without significant injury to their drugs' reputations.

Controversy about SSRIs' side effects flared into national prominence . . . in 2004 when they and older antidepressants were shown to double the risk of suicidal thoughts and behavior in children and adolescents. That discovery prompted the FDA to slap a stern "black box" warning on the drugs' package inserts. (Among other things, it cautions doctors to monitor young patients closely in their first months on SSRIs.)

A black-box warning about suicidal thoughts and behavior in adults may very well be next, say a number of experts interviewed by *Fortune*. "I'm fully expecting that the same [risk found in young patients] will be found in adults," says Dr. Richard Kapit, an ex-FDA official who handled the agency's first safety review of Prozac before its approval in 1987. (He now works as a medical writer and consultant in Bethesda, Md.) In fact, last summer the FDA warned that several recent studies suggest that SSRIs and other antidepressants raise the risk of suicidal behavior in adults as well as kids. The agency added that it is reviewing "all available data" on the issue in an investigation expected to take a year or more.

Risk of suicide isn't the only problem dogging SSRIs. For example, GlaxoSmithKline faces thousands of lawsuits on another side effect, severe withdrawal reactions to its drug Paxil, one of the fastest-acting SSRIs. Last year British policymakers moved to discourage the use of SSRIs to treat mild depression. And a recent scientific analysis has challenged long-held assumptions about how the drugs work. That could undercut drugmakers' assertions that SSRIs are well understood, potentially increasing doubts about their safety.

A black-box warning for adults could have huge repercussions, vaporizing billions of dollars of future sales, increasing pressure on policymakers to curtail direct-to-consumer drug ads, and prompting a slew of lawsuits. It could also complicate drugmakers' efforts to roll out new antidepressants to replace current ones as the drugs go off patent. The ultimate fallout could well equal or exceed that from Vioxx, the Merck painkiller whose saga of potentially lethal risks, dodgy marketing, and damaging courtroom disclosures has given Big Pharma the look of an ethical disaster zone. If so, it would add a sad twist to a tale in which so many people have been helped.

## Birth of a Blockbuster

Prozac and its kin have been one of 20th-century medicine's great success stories. Since the debut of Eli Lilly's Prozac in 1988, the drugs have grown into an $11-billion-a-year market in the U.S. alone. Nearly 150 million U.S. prescriptions were dispensed in 2004 for SSRIs and similar antidepressants called SNRIs, according to IMS Health, a Fairfield, Conn., drug data and consulting company—more than for any other drug except codeine. Perhaps one out of 20 adult Americans are on them now, making brands like Zoloft, GlaxoSmithKline's Paxil, Forest Laboratories' Celexa, and Solvay Pharmaceuticals' Luvox household names. Though they don't work for everybody—many people have gone off the medicines because of side effects such as dampening of sexual response—they've done more than any other class of drugs to spur psychiatry's substitution of pills for couches.

In fact, we're popping so many SSRIs that their breakdown products in urine, gushing into waterways, have accumulated in fish tissues, raising concerns that aquatic animals may be getting toxic doses, according to recent research at Baylor University.

The SSRI phenomenon began almost the minute Prozac appeared. Doctors embraced the drugs because of a virtue that seems increasingly ironic: It's hard to commit suicide by overdosing on SSRIs, so they are deemed safer to give to severely depressed patients than are older, more acutely toxic antidepressants such as the so-called tricyclics. Indeed, the drugs once seemed so benign that some psychiatrists marveled about how they appear to violate the law of "conservation of mood"—a seemingly universal pattern in which drug-induced emotional lifts are always followed by crashes, resulting in no net gain. Such talk made Prozac seem safer than coffee. That paved the way for massive prescribing by general practitioners with no special training in complex mental disorders—in recent years some 70% of SSRI prescriptions have been written by primary-care doctors.

---

*The drugs may actually create a perilous brain imbalance in some people.*

---

Within three years of Prozac's launch, annual sales neared $800 million. *Newsweek* put the pill on its cover—a green-and-white capsule floating against a blue sky under a headline that hailed it as a breakthrough drug. Even healthy people were asking for Prozac, the magazine noted. By 1993 the idea caught on that SSRIs could transform lives—curing not only depression but also shyness, low self-esteem, and compulsiveness. Major boosts for the fad came from *Listening to Prozac*, psychiatrist Peter Kramer's eloquent bestseller, and from celebrity endorsements. Recounting his fight with depression, Mike Wallace of CBS's *60 Minutes* told *Newsweek* he expected to take Zoloft for the rest of his life.

## The Dark Side

But for all the glow about SSRIs, the drugs have been among the most controversial in the history of medicine. Bitter disputes about side effects have seethed for more than a decade, usually out of sight of the mainstream media—in supermarket tabloids, on websites, and in professional gatherings of scientists, regulators, and shrinks.

Rare, dangerous side effects of potent medicines like antidepressants often emerge only after the drugs have been prescribed to millions of people for years. But in the case of SSRIs, that is not the whole story. There are signs that manufacturers have downplayed known risks of the lucrative drugs and that regulators and doctors haven't been skeptical enough about them.

Even the theoretical basis for prescribing SSRIs is now in doubt. The drugs have long been said to work by boosting a brain chemical called serotonin, correcting a neural imbalance underlying depression and other ills. That makes them seem the epitome of modern medicine—what could be safer than restoring a natural balance? A growing body of studies casts doubt on the theory, however, according to a provocative report this month in *PLoS Medicine*, an influential peer-reviewed journal published by the nonprofit Public Library of Science. The report points out that scientists have never really understood the drugs' effects in the brain. Yet pharmaceutical ads still cite the serotonin theory as a major reason for prescribing SSRIs—a case of mythmaking "comparable to the masturbatory theory of insanity," says British psychiatrist David Healy, a longtime SSRI critic. Drug company spokesmen counter that considerable scientific literature supports the serotonin-imbalance idea.

A number of scientists have theorized that while boosting serotonin, SSRIs indirectly inhibit another key neurochemical messenger called dopamine. That means the drugs may actually create a perilous brain imbalance in some people. What's more, there's some evidence that dopamine inhibition underlies several of the rare, serious side effects linked to SSRIs. One is akathisia, a kind of extreme restlessness that has been implicated in suicidal impulses—Witczak believes Zoloft induced akathisia in her husband.

The possibility that SSRIs may occasionally induce deranged mental states conducive to homicide has cropped up again and again in the news. While evidence supporting that idea is scanty compared with data on the risk of suicidal ideas and behavior, it isn't easily dismissed out of hand. Consider some of the testimony at the trial this year of teenager Christopher Pittman, charged with murdering his grandparents. Richard Kapit, the ex-FDA official, testified for the defense—he says he felt compelled to come forward after reading about the case in the news. Kapit told the jury that the teen was "involuntarily intoxicated" by SSRIs when he shot his grandparents. Kapit added that he believes that Pittman, who was being tried as an adult and who was ultimately found guilty, "didn't have the ability to form criminal intent" when he committed the murders at age 12.

## Seeing the Big Picture on SSRIs

Many psychiatrists feel that stories about SSRIs' side effects should themselves carry bold cautions against media hype. The risk noted in the FDA black-box warning is limited: Suicidal thoughts and behaviors occurred in about 4% of youngsters on antidepressants (mostly SSRIs) in clinical trials, vs. 2% of those taking dummy pills. That doesn't necessarily mean actual suicides occur more often among SSRI takers—there's too little data to answer that question. And the risk must be balanced against the fact that SSRIs help many people—no one disputes that depression is a huge problem, and even some of SSRIs' harshest critics concede the drugs can play a valuable role in treating it when prescribed judiciously.

The uproar, in fact, may be hurting some patients without access to psychotherapy, the main alternative to drugs. Since family doctors are now often afraid to prescribe SSRIs to kids, more depressed young people than ever are probably going untreated, says Gregory Simon, a psychiatrist and health-care policy researcher at Group Health Cooperative, a Seattle HMO. Prescriptions of antidepressants for patients 18 and under have plunged by 20% since the suicide issue hit headlines in early 2004, according to NDCHealth, an Atlanta health-care information provider. (Less than 5% of antidepressant prescriptions are written for youngsters.) Says Jerrold Rosenbaum, psychiatrist-in-chief at Boston's Massachusetts General Hospital: "Most of us [in psychiatry] think the number of patients harmed by failure to treat [due to fear of SSRIs] is much higher than the number who are harmed by treatment."

*Drug marketers have been extraordinarily adept at selling SSRIs—even to people who may not need them.*

Of course, many top U.S. psychiatrists, including Dr. Rosenbaum, have worked with drug companies to establish SSRIs as medicines of choice for treating depression. Their views aren't universal in medicine—European authorities have long been more skeptical about the drugs. Soon after the FDA approved Prozac for marketing in December 1987, German regulators rejected it, partly because of concerns that the drug increased the risk of suicide; they later approved it but required Lilly to include a warning in the drug's package insert about the possible need to prescribe sedatives to counter the risk. [In] December [2004], Britain's National Institute for Clinical Excellence, which guides that country's health-care policy, recommended that SSRIs and other antidepressants not be prescribed "for the initial treatment of mild depression, because the risk-benefit ratio is poor."

And in April [2005] the British House of Commons Health Committee issued a caustic report that may give a preview of things to come in Congress. SSRIs have been "indiscriminately prescribed on a grand scale," the committee concluded, partly due to "data secrecy and uncritical acceptance of drug company views." Further, industry promotions have "worked to persuade too many professionals that they can prescribe [the drugs] with impunity" to treat "unhappiness [that] is part of the spectrum of human experience, not a medical condition." Though Congress isn't likely to buy into the stiff-upper-lip rationale, it may put some very awkward questions about SSRIs to their makers and the FDA. . . . (Texas Republican Joe Barton and other Congressmen grilled FDA officials for hours just before the agency put the black-box warning on SSRIs for kids.)

## Clever Marketing

Drug marketers have been extraordinarily adept at selling SSRIs—even to people who may not need them. Consider that the drugs, once limited to treating major depression, are now prescribed for everything from shyness about peeing in public restrooms to shopoholism. (Such uses aren't approved by the FDA, but there's no law against doctors prescribing SSRIs and other drugs for "off label" indications.)

---

*Doctors, insurers, regulators—and we eager pill-poppers—are all co-conspirators.*

---

The explosive growth of the drugs' market is largely a story of clever branding as makers of "me too" SSRIs sought to replicate Prozac's success. Pfizer, for example, positioned Zoloft, launched in 1992, as a versatile antidepressant that could also treat ills such as post-traumatic stress disorder. Glaxo targeted Paxil, launched in 1993, at anxiety disorders such as SAD (social anxiety disorder, or excessive shyness) and GAD (generalized anxiety disorder, or unremitting angst)—ills that had received little attention before Glaxo began promoting Paxil to treat them. Lilly countered by expanding Prozac's indications to include PMDD (premenstrual dysphoric disorder, or very bad moods some women suffer before their periods) and depression in children.

Indeed, to marketers, SSRIs have been the pharmaceutical equivalent of Play-Doh. In a remarkably forthright 2003 article, Vince Parry, now a branding expert at Ventiv Health, a Somerset, N.J., health-care marketing firm, waxed euphoric about psychiatry's "ownable syndromes." Published in a trade journal, the article laid out strategies "for fostering the creation of a [medical] condition and aligning it with a product" like an SSRI. Wrote Parry: "No therapeutic category is more accepting of condition branding than the field of anxiety and depression, where illness is rarely based on measurable physical symptoms." He cites Lilly's positioning of Prozac to treat premenstrual woe as an excellent example of condition branding—the company reinvigorated its aging antidepressant by repackaging it in a lavender pill, dubbed Sarafem, for women with PMDD.

But blaming marketers alone for the SSRI fad isn't fair. Doctors, insurers, regulators—and we eager pill-poppers—are co-conspirators. Cupertino, Calif., resident Ada Spade, for instance, takes an SSRI for a condition that even few psychiatrists know about: compulsive shopping. The problem started about 15 years ago when she was in her 30s, she says. "I'd go to the grocery store and find myself stopping at eight stores on the way to buy something in every one of them. I just could not stop." She tried therapy, budgeting, cash-only purchasing—nothing had lasting effect. Her life changed a few years ago when she took part in a study at Stanford University Medical Center. Funded by Forest Laboratories, it showed that 17 of 24 "compulsive shoppers" given Celexa, an SSRI made by Forest, were greatly improved—they could even visit malls without buying anything. "I learned from the study," she says, "that, yeah, something is a little wrong with me, but with medication I can be okay."

For harried doctors faced with lots of patients complaining of depression, anxiety, or compulsions, drugs billed as versatile and safe can seem a godsend. Prescribing SSRIs "has almost become a way that physicians are regulating demands on their time," says University of Pennsylvania psychology professor James Coyne. "What happens a lot in primary care, though, is that people on the drugs don't get adequate follow-up. About half the time they need an adjustment in dose, which they often don't get," increasing the chance of side effects.

That effectively means a double whammy of risk: It raises the odds that rare patients vulnerable to dangerous reactions will get the drugs as well as the chance that they will spin out of control unmonitored by doctors. Even when patients are monitored, emerging suicidal tendencies are often missed, says Jerome Vaccaro, CEO of PacifiCare Behavioral Health, a mental-health-benefits manager in Santa Ana, Calif. "It's a 'don't ask, don't tell' problem," he says. "Doctors don't ask about it, and patients don't spontaneously volunteer they're feeling suicidal." To SSRI critics, these nitty-gritty considerations should have prompted sterner warnings years ago. Asserts psychiatrist Joseph Glenmullen: "The problem is that when you give these drugs to a large population, you can get lethal side effects."

---

*The real scandal [about SSRIs] has been the failure to disclose data.*

---

## Mother's Little Helpers

If one had to identify when the sea change on SSRIs started, April 2000 would be a top candidate. That's when Glenmullen, a clinical instructor at Harvard who also works for its student health service, published a book called *Prozac Backlash*. Playing up SSRI side effects via scary patient vignettes, the book has become to the drugs' bashers what *Listening to Prozac* was to their fans. Glenmullen sipped tea recently at a Cambridge, Mass., coffee shop while laying out provocative historical parallels for the rise and possible fall of SSRIs.

Drug fads in psychiatry, he says, have appeared "like clockwork" in 30-year cycles. The first was cocaine elixirs, which doctors in the late 1800s prescribed for everything from depression to shyness. Freud bolstered the fad by commending cocaine in influential papers. But by the 1920s, cocaine's dangers had become clear, and amphetamines replaced it as psychiatric cure-alls. In the late 1930s uppers like Benzedrine were even sold over the counter to treat nasal congestion. After the dangers of amphetamines rose to the fore, the pattern was repeated with barbiturates and later with habit-forming tranquilizers such as Valium. (Remember "mother's little helpers," from the Rolling Stones song in the 1960s?)

Each fad followed the same trajectory. The medicines were first hailed as wonder drugs for major mental illnesses. Then general practitioners began prescribing them not just for major problems but for all sorts of relatively minor maladies. Next, scattered reports of serious side effects appeared. After 20 years or so of use, sellers of the medicines could no longer plausibly deny the problems, leading finally to sharply curtailed prescribing. Given that SSRIs' popularity took off in 1990, Glenmullen predicts that "we're still five to ten years away" from full disenchantment with them.

Very few doctors agree with his view that SSRIs are as problematic as, say, amphetamines. But a number of his positions—such as the charge that drug companies have selectively used clinical trial data on SSRIs to paint an overly rosy picture of them—no longer seem radical. Says Group Health's Dr. Simon: "The real scandal [about SSRIs] has been the failure to disclose data." Take the revelations that led the FDA to impose the black-box warning about prescribing SSRIs for kids. The story began in 2003 when FDA officials noticed a curious thing while examining the results of a trial with youngsters on Glaxo's Paxil: The company reported that substantially more kids had shown "emotional lability" on the drug than on a placebo.

Emotional lability? When the officials asked what the term meant, Glaxo submitted details showing that "almost all of these events related to suicidality," according to an FDA internal e-mail on the matter in June 2003. (Suicidality is shrink-speak for suicidal ideas or actions; the e-mail was eventually made public at a congressional hearing but got scant media attention.) The implication of higher suicidality on Paxil "has us worried," the FDA's Dr. Russell Katz noted in the message, which he sent to colleague Dr. Andrew Mosholder, an expert on drug safety. Glaxo, he noted acidly, "has not proposed labeling changes [on Paxil to reflect the discovery], and makes a feeble attempt to dismiss the finding." Agency officials launched a massive reexamination of trial data on antidepressants in children.

That inquiry turned up worrisome data on suicide-related risk—information that caused internal dissension at the FDA. Just before an FDA advisory panel hearing on the issue, the *San Francisco Chronicle* reported that senior agency officials had forbidden Mosholder to go public with his findings on the risk. The agency's top brass feared that the data, which were still tentative, might discourage doctors from giving antidepressants to kids who needed them. But the focus of criticism soon shifted back to Glaxo. In June 2004, New York Attorney General Eliot Spitzer sued the company, alleging that it had fraudulently withheld unfavorable data on youngsters treated with Paxil. (Glaxo, which asserts that the lawsuit was "unfounded," settled by agreeing to post its clinical results on the web.) In October [2004] the FDA finally confirmed that the suicide-related risk is real for a wide array of antidepressants and required the stern warning on their labels.

## Clean Bill of Health?

For years, FDA officials had reason to be perplexed. SSRI makers have long maintained there's no reliable scientific evidence that SSRIs cause suicidal or aggressive behavior. Other key factors, like mind-boggling medical complexity, helped obscure the issue. For instance, depression itself can increase suicidal thoughts and behaviors, which makes it extremely difficult to tell whether a drug is to blame. Further, doctors have long believed that antidepressants sometimes "energize" depressed patients before lifting their moods—potentially making them more prone to enact their despair. But over the past 15 years critics have amassed a small mountain of data that point to suicide-related side effects, including reams of medical journal reports, internal FDA memorandums obtained with Freedom of Information Act filings, and unpublished industry documents pried out via discovery in lawsuits.

The commotion about suicide risks dates back to 1990, when Harvard psychiatrist Martin Teicher and colleagues reported that six of their depressed patients had developed "intense, violent suicidal preoccupation" soon after starting on Prozac. The report sparked sensational media stories on the drug's purported dangers. But studies soon made the case that Prozac is no more dangerous than older antidepressants and possibly much safer. The scare was further deflated by revelations that the anti-psychiatry Church of Scientology had helped promote it. In September 1991, an FDA advisory panel concluded there was "no credible evidence" that Prozac promotes suicidal or violent impulses.

---

*There's definitely a reluctance by the FDA to come out and say, "A drug we've approved is really dangerous."*

---

A far less reassuring analysis had unfolded behind the scenes, according to internal FDA documents. The documents were later obtained by attorneys representing plaintiffs who sued Lilly, alleging that Prozac had triggered suicidal and violent acts. Lilly has quietly paid an estimated $50 million–plus to settle more than 30 such suits, according to an investigation in 2000 by the *Indianapolis Star*. "Any settlements were based upon business decisions," says Lilly spokesman Dan Collins. "We do not comment on specific details regarding lawsuits."

A few months after Teicher's report, an FDA safety official [named David Graham] wrote to his superiors sharply criticizing a study Lilly had submitted to the agency in hopes of quelling the suicide concerns.... His 1990 memo about Prozac argued that Lilly's "analysis of suicidality does not resolve the issue" because the company had excluded cases of patients who weren't in the company's main clinical trials—Graham had access to data from early Prozac studies that were separate from the ones the drugmakers emphasized. "It can be argued that these exclusions are not justified or appropriate," he wrote. This "apparent large-scale underreporting" of patients with "treatment-emergent suicidality" meant Lilly had not proved that Prozac and violent behavior are unrelated, he argued. Yet when it came time for the FDA to conduct the crucial hearing in 1991, Graham's analysis wasn't mentioned and Prozac was exonerated. The clean bill of health is well deserved, Lilly maintains. "More than 54 million patients worldwide have taken Prozac," says Collins; it's "among the most studied medications in history," and its safety "is thoroughly documented."

Yet critics blame the FDA's response largely on coziness between the agency and Big Pharma—and on senior officials' fear of looking careless. Says Kapit: "There's definitely a reluctance by the FDA to come out and say, 'A drug we've approved is really dangerous.'" The problem is compounded, he adds, by the fact that the FDA unit charged with monitoring drugs' post-launch safety is subsumed under the FDA branch that oversees drug approvals. The drug-safety office has no autonomy to go public with its findings. If it could, Graham's analysis of the Prozac data might have come out as early as 1991. (The FDA did not respond to repeated requests for comment.)

## An Injection of Itching Powder

SSRIs' darkest side may be the suicide risk. But other adverse effects may pose just as big a problem for drugmakers. In the mid-1990s, for example, horror stories about SSRI withdrawal symptoms began circulating on the Internet, signaling a controversy that is now nearly as bitter as the one about suicide. One of its leading crusaders, Rob Robinson, a building contractor in Signal Mountain, Tenn., recently organized a protest against GlaxoSmithKline at its U.S. headquarters in Philadelphia. He held a BOYCOTT GLAXOSMITHKLINE sign as he paced the sidewalk in front of the high-rise building along with a handful of fellow protesters.

A rock climber of renown—*Climbing* magazine once put him on its cover—Robinson, 45, says his experience with SSRIs started in 1998. He had committed to do a traveling exhibition on climbing, but the project stressed him out and interfered with his sleep, so his doctor prescribed Glaxo's Paxil. After a few weeks on the drug, Robinson says, "I felt calmer. I thought, 'That's good.'" Quitting it after a half-year, though, "I started having what I now know are withdrawal symptoms," he asserts, including muscle spasms, extreme sensitivity to sound, and "horrible electric-shock sensations in my head." He went back on Paxil to alleviate the symptoms. Eventually concluding he had a drug dependency, he found a specialist who took him off the drug in 18 days. That triggered severe symptoms that Robinson claims brought him to the brink of suicide. "I finally opened a door at the far side of hell after about 18 months," he says.

Today Robinson runs a website on Paxil's risks and has sued Glaxo, charging that it deliberately failed to warn about the drug's potential to cause severe withdrawal symptoms. Some 3,000 similar suits against Glaxo have been filed across the country over the past few years, says Karen Barth Menzies, an attorney at Baum Hedlund, a Los Angeles law firm that has handled many SSRI-related suits.

Glaxo's drug has become the withdrawal issue's main lightning rod because it washes out of the body more quickly than most other SSRIs. Hence the effects of its absence in the brain can occur with literally dizzying speed. (Doctors recommend gradually tapering doses before quitting to minimize such symptoms.) The symptoms of SSRI "discontinuation syndrome," as psychiatrists call it, include dizziness, headaches, nausea, lethargy, insomnia, irritability, visual disturbances, movement disorders, and electric-shock sensations (known as "electric head" on web chat groups about SSRIs).

Glaxo concedes that such symptoms may occur when people quit taking Paxil abruptly. Discontinuation symptoms, a spokeswoman notes, can also occur with other medicines, such as blood-pressure drugs. But she says allegations that Paxil is addictive, or that Glaxo has tried to hide data on side effects, are groundless. Most discontinuation symptoms, she adds, are "mild to moderate in intensity, resolve on their own within two weeks, and seldom need corrective therapy." It remains to be seen how well such assertions will play in a courtroom if the withdrawal lawsuits, which are still in pretrial proceedings, aren't settled first.

The most consequential SSRI side-effects lawsuit on the industry's horizon, however, appears to be the Witczak case against Pfizer—the one involving the man who hanged himself after taking Zoloft. The symptoms Woody Witczak purportedly experienced suggest the restlessness-causing condition called akathisia. It was first linked to the antidepressants in the 1980s; critics like Glenmullen assert that it is one of SSRIs' most dangerous side effects, in part because it is rarely seen, hence easily missed, by general practitioners who prescribe the drugs. Ironically, a former Pfizer researcher wrote one of the medical literature's most detailed articles on the subject while working for the company. His report, which appeared in the *Journal of Psychopharmacology* in 1998, states that SSRIs "may occasionally induce" akathisia. The condition's name comes from the Greek for "not sitting still," and its cardinal symptom is intense jitters—a patient who has experienced the sensation compares it to an intravenous injection of itching powder. Akathisia is so unbearable for some depressed patients on SSRIs that they apparently feel "death is a welcome result," according to the report.

CURRENT
CONTROVERSIES

CHAPTER 3

# What Are Alternative Treatments for Mental Illness?

# Chapter Preface

Because mental health is so complex, and is influenced by life experience as well as biological vulnerabilities one inherits, it is not surprising that approaches to treating mental illness are so diverse and often divergent. One person with depression may benefit from a year on an antidepressant and move on to a productive, happy life, while another might take yoga classes and see an acupuncturist for relief. Yet another might take a ballroom dancing course and a course of St. John's wort, an herb long used to treat depression, which has been found by numerous studies to be as effective as antidepressants.

For mental illnesses like severe bipolar disorder and schizophrenia, which both involve a strong genetic contribution and a known brain action that causes them, as well as for severe clinical depression, there is less variation in treatment—the treatment of choice is often medication a person takes for his or her lifetime, although alternative approaches can play a significant role in improving quality of life for patients, and perhaps reducing how much medication they need. But in the case of anxiety disorders as well as what is known as unipolar depression, which is characterized by sadness and irritability (while bipolar disorder has a manic [hyperexcited] component as well), experts disagree about the degree to which these conditions are inherited, and whether a specific brain activity causes them, so there is a lot more flexibility in how to treat them.

What many, though not all, of the non-drug approaches to achieving mental wellness have in common is greater emphasis on active participation of the person who has a problem. Martin Seligman, Director of the Positive Psychology Center at the University of Pennsylvania, thinks such active participation in the process of achieving good mental health is essential to combating the victimology that has become pervasive in society over the past 40 years—and that he thinks may be related to continued high levels of depression. This culture tends to support the belief that mental illness is inflicted on people by some larger force, but this view leads to passivity and helplessness, according to Seligman. "You are not a passive responder to stimuli," he said in an interview in *EQ Today: Learning, Love, and Leadership through Emotional Intelligence.* "You are an initiator of plans. A lot of your troubles were brought on by yourself. You are responsible for them. And the good news in that it also implies that the way out is not something that someone is going to bestow on you; it's something you are going to do yourself."

Talk therapy, including cognitive therapy described in this chapter, involves a great deal of effort by the person participating in it (including homework!), as does participating in regular physical exercise, neurofeedback, creating habits of good nutrition, and building on good relationships and community support—all approaches known to buffet humans from some of the slings and arrows of life. This chapter describes some of these approaches, as well as vagus nerve therapy, a novel type of electrical brain stimulation that may help those suffering from severe depression when other approaches have failed.

# Exercise Provides Benefits for the Mentally Ill

*Abby Ellin*

*Abby Ellin is a writer and author of* Teenage Waistland: A Former Fat Kid Weighs in on Living Large, Losing Weight, and How Parents Can (and Can't) Help.

Matthew Hass is not sure what caused him to blow up to 300 pounds: his sedentary lifestyle, a diet devoid of fruits or vegetables or the medications he took for bipolar disorder. Not that the cause mattered. Mr. Hass knew he was at a crossroads: at 27 he said he felt like a "heart attack waiting to happen," so he decided to give exercise a chance. "I was ready to try something else that would help my moods," he said, "and maybe help me lose some weight too."

Mr. Hass, now 28, began working out with a personal trainer on Fridays, thanks to a program in Keene, N.H., called In Shape that pairs people with severe mental illnesses with mentors to guide them through a fitness regime. For almost a year and a half he also did circuit training and played tennis with his mentor. Since he signed up for In Shape not only has he lost 30 pounds, but he said his moods are steadier.

His experience illustrates why mental health experts increasingly recommend exercise for people with severe mental illness. It helps them stay physically healthy, which is crucial in a population that the surgeon general estimated in 1999 loses on average 15.4 years' life expectancy. And research suggests that by improving mood, exercise can be a beneficial accompaniment to other kinds of treatment for mental illness. While exercise is unlikely ever to replace medication and psychotherapy, experts say, it can increase the likelihood that those traditional strategies will be effective.

Scientists have long known that exercise lifts the spirits of people without mental illness, and hundreds of studies have shown how it can improve the psychological health of those who suffer moderate depression, whether or not they take medication or engage in talk therapy.

## Empowering the Mentally Ill

But newer research has looked specifically at what good exercise can do for people with conditions like bipolar disorder, schizophrenia and severe anxiety disorders. In a recent study at Boston University, for example, 15 previously sedentary patients suffering from mood or psychotic disorders exercised with an instructor three times a week. After three months they reported that their symptoms of depression had lessened, and that they felt a sense of empowerment they had not known before.

A similar study, at the University of Florida College of Nursing at Gainesville, looked at the effects of an aerobic exercise program on 20 people with schizophrenia. After four months of working out three times a week, the patients lost weight and gained cardiovascular fitness. And compared with a control group of sedentary patients, the exercisers also had fewer psychiatric symptoms, like social withdrawal and paranoia.

Mental health experts, already concerned about their patients' weight and inactivity, have been spurred by such research to encourage patients to work out. Many have started programs like In Shape to help people with severe mental illness get moving.

"More and more people in the field are looking at this because people with mental illness are dropping dead from things that are lifestyle related," like a lack of exercise and poor nutrition, said Dori Hutchinson, the executive director of services at the Center for Psychiatric Rehabilitation, a research center at Boston University that recently began a four-day-a-week program. Patients walk, stretch and lift weights with a trainer and once a week play basketball or soccer. They also learn about nutrition and cooking.

At Fountain House in Manhattan people with schizophrenia and bipolar disorder get together to do yoga or tai chi three times a week or to walk for an hour or two. Last month McLean Hospital, a psychiatric hospital in Belmont, Mass., opened a fitness center with cardiovascular and strength training equipment. Soon yoga and aerobics classes will be added. "Ideally we'd like them to go most days for an hour," said Sally Jenks, the director of business development at the hospital.

In Shape, which began two years ago, is one of the more established exercise programs for the mentally ill. After going to a spate of funerals for relatively young patients, Ken Jue, the chief executive of Monadnock Family Services, a community mental health center in Keene, created the program to help patients lead longer and healthier lives.

## Mental Illness Compromises Physical Health

"Their physical health is compromised," Mr. Jue explained, "partly due to side effects of prescribed medications, partly due to the impact of mental illness on lifestyle choices, and in part due to economic limitations that many people with mental illness experience."

*I have people with schizophrenia who swim half a mile. [. . .] They sleep better, they have less anxiety, and they're less depressed. Do they still hear voices? Yes, but the exercise helps them cope.*

Initially he had hoped to attract 40 people; 65 signed up. They work out as much as they want with a personal trainer and in groups. They are also taught the basics of cooking and nutrition, as well as smoking cessation. The goal is to get patients into the habit of exercising regularly on their own, as Mr. Hass does. These days he walks an hour a day and lifts weights three times a week.

Ann Lapointe, 37, joined the In Shape program in May. At that time, she said, "I was sleeping all the time, couldn't clean the house, couldn't take care of my 9-year-old son." Now she hikes or lifts weights with her mentor for 90 minutes once a week. Other days she takes aerobics or spinning classes.

"It's really important for elevating my mood," said Ms. Lapointe, who suffers from bipolar, obsessive compulsive and anxiety disorders. She said she relies on her mentor's encouragement. "To be praised for exercising really helps."

Mr. Hass is feeling so much better that he no longer takes the eight medications he took for his bipolar disorder before he started exercising. He is down to just one drug, and he attributes that to regular workouts.

Most doctors say that exercise can never replace drugs, however, and that should never be the goal.

"It would be a mistake to think exercise can be used instead of other treatments for depression," said Dr. Norman Sussman, a psychiatrist at New York University Medical Center.

## Better Coping Through Exercise

Although exercise can be beneficial for people with schizophrenia, these patients must still take their medications, said Dr. Ken Duckworth, the medical director of the National Alliance on Mental Illness in Boston. "I have people with schizophrenia who swim half a mile," he explained. "They sleep better, they have less anxiety and they're less depressed. Do they still hear voices? Yes. But exercise helps them cope."

In some cases, Dr. Sussman noted, exercise is impractical. "If someone is so apathetic that they can't even change their clothes or get out of bed, which happens in severe depression, how can you tell them to go down to the *health* club?"

Some personal trainers specialize in helping the mentally ill get moving. Jeff Rutstein in Boston works with many people who have schizophrenia or bipolar disorder. Over the last few years his business has grown in part because he is often sent doctor referrals from McLean Hospital.

"I get them to focus on their specific muscle group instead of on their negative thoughts," Mr. Rutstein said.

Marie Cotton, who is 60 and has suffered from depression for decades, is one of his clients. When she first got on the treadmill, Mrs. Cotton, a travel agent, said she was terribly afraid of falling. "Jeff always gave me a sense of security that he would not let me get hurt, which was a huge, huge thing."

Working out twice a week has helped Mrs. Cotton cope with her illness. She said she prefers Mr. Rutstein's private gym to group exercise. "You're not on display," she added.

Part of what Mr. Hass likes about the In Shape program is its anonymity. Patients work out at the YMCA among other fitness enthusiasts, and nobody knows who is in the program and who is not. And although mentors are willing to talk about clients' medical problems, that is not their focus.

"They are not their mental illness," said Brenda Buffum, 30, the lead health mentor for In Shape. "I treat them like any other training client."

# Cognitive Therapy Is Effective at Treating Depression

## The Economist

The Economist *is a weekly newspaper focusing on international politics, business news, and opinion.*

For almost a century after Sigmund Freud pioneered psychoanalysis, "talk therapy" was the treatment of choice for many mental illnesses. Artists and writers lined up to lie down and be analysed, and the ideas of Freud, Jung, and other influential psychiatrists permeated the intellectual world. They also seeped into the popular consciousness, and still pop up today whenever someone talks of a subconscious desire, a Freudian slip, a death wish, or an Oedipal complex. But advances in neurology, and especially in pharmacology, have called such therapy into question. When psychological and emotional disturbances can be traced to faulty brain chemistry and corrected with a pill, the idea that sitting and talking can treat a problem such as clinical depression might seem outdated.

Robert DeRubeis of the University of Pennsylvania and his colleagues beg to differ, however. They have conducted the largest clinical trial ever designed to compare talk therapy with chemical antidepressants. The result, just published in *Archives of General Psychiatry*, is that talking works as well as pills do. Indeed, it works better, if you take into account the lower relapse rate.

The study looked at a relatively modern type of talk therapy, known as cognitive therapy, which tries to teach people how to change harmful thoughts and beliefs. Patients learn to recognise unrealistically negative thoughts when they occur, and are told how to replace them with more positive ones. It may sound too simplistic to work, but other studies have shown it can be used to treat anxiety, obsessive-compulsive disorder and eating disorders. Dr DeRubeis wondered just how effective it really was for depression.

In the study, 240 patients with moderate to severe depression were divided into three groups. One group was treated with cognitive therapy, a second with Paxil, an antidepressant drug, and members of the third group were given placebo pills. (Those in the second and third groups did not know whether their pills were placebos or not.) After 16 weeks of treatment, the results for those on cognitive therapy and drugs were identical. Some 58% had shown perceptible improvement. By contrast, only 25% of those on the placebo improved. That was encouraging. But the really surprising advantage of cognitive therapy is that it seems to keep working even after the therapy sessions are over. A year after treatments ended, only 31% of those who had received it had relapsed into their former state, while 76% of those who had been given antidepressants, and then been taken off them, had done so. Even patients who stayed on antidepressants for the intervening year did not do any better than those who had taken cognitive therapy and then quit.

If Dr DeRubeis's study can be replicated (an important "if" in a soft-edged discipline such as psychotherapy), it has implications for the way clinical depression should be approached in the future. One consideration, at least in America, where the study was done, is that many medical-insurance companies that are willing to pay for antidepressant drugs nevertheless refuse to pay for psychotherapy. A successful replication of the DeRubeis study ought to change that—not least because cost-benefit analysis shows that while cognitive therapy is more expensive than drug treatment to start with (since it involves extended one-to-one sessions with a highly paid specialist), it is cheaper in the long run because prescriptions do not have to be refilled indefinitely.

Which is not to say that cognitive therapy will suit everyone with depression. According to Dr DeRubeis, it is still likely that some patients will respond better to drugs than conversation. The next breakthrough might be a way of working out in advance who fits which treatment.

# Neurofeedback Training Can Help Treat Mental Disorders

*Jody Jaffe*

*Jody Jaffe is a writer whose articles have appeared in publications including the* New York Times, *the* Los Angeles Times, *and* Washingtonian.

When Lori told Jeff, her 15-year-old son, to write up his *Odyssey* notes for English class, he ran to the kitchen and grabbed a knife. He pointed it at himself, then turned it on his mother.

"If you won't let me kill myself," he screamed, "I'll kill you."

He fell to the floor and cradled his head between his hands. "I can't stop it! My head, my head," he said as he rocked back and forth.

That was in the spring of 2003. Lori couldn't remember a time when her younger son had been happy. Prone to violent behavior, he'd been in psychotherapy since age 11. He'd been on three types of medications and tried individual and group therapy. Nothing was working.

"I know what hell looks like," says the 48-year-old Springfield mother of three. "It's your child. . . ." She struggles to finish the sentence. "This time two years ago, I would have sworn to you I was going to be burying my child. He wanted out, and he was planning it."

Then Dr. Michael Anderson, a McLean psychiatrist, suggested Jeff try neurofeedback training. It had helped Anderson's daughter with her attention deficit disorder as well as many of his patients who hadn't responded to medication for other problems.

Jody Jaffe, "Pumping Neurons," *Washingtonian*, January 2006. Copyright 2006 Washington Magazine, Inc. Reproduced by permission of the author.

On Anderson's recommendation, Lori took Jeff to Deborah Stokes, an Alexandria neurofeedback therapist.

"I was skeptical of it because I'd tried a lot of things and nothing seemed to work," says Jeff. "Every day was a battle, emotional and physical."

After 15 sessions, he noticed a difference: "I wasn't as stressed out and depressed."

After 45 sessions, his mother noticed big changes. "He's happy; he smiles," Lori says. "He's off antidepressants for the first time since fourth grade.

"He's got a life ahead of him, where I didn't think he had one before."

---

*Though neurofeedback therapy has been available for more than 25 years, it's only recently started to attract mainstream attention.*

---

## A Brain Gym

Jeff's story was one of many I heard while researching neurofeedback training and another brain therapy, EEG (electroencephalogram) stimulation. A Northern Virginia boy with Tourette's syndrome saw his tics almost disappear; a man with Lyme disease can now sleep through the night; a musician with debilitating headaches is not only pain-free but hears the bass notes better; several Montgomery County golfers are playing better; and 30 students at London's Royal College of Music scored a full grade higher on performance exams during a study of neurofeedback training, which is now part of the college's curriculum.

I have a story of my own, though it is not as dramatic as Jeff's. I can find my keys.

Neurofeedback training is a kind of biofeedback therapy. But instead of learning to control body temperature or muscle tension, as with traditional biofeedback, you learn to control your brain waves.

It started in the late 1960s with cats and rocket fuel. M. Barry Sterman, a UCLA sleep researcher, discovered that a kind of brain wave, SMR, or sensorimotor response, was associated with a reduction of muscle tension in cats. He taught some cats to increase the frequency of this brain wave.

Right after that study, NASA asked him to research the toxic effects of the rocket fuel monomethyl hydrazine. Among the test cats were some who'd been trained to increase their SMR waves. After being exposed to the fuel, those cats didn't have seizures.

Sterman then tested people with epilepsy who weren't responding to medication. He found a 60-percent reduction in seizures for those who were taught to increase the SMR brainwave frequency. Researchers soon found that controlling brain waves worked in all sorts of situations.

Though neurofeedback therapy has been available for more than 25 years, it's only recently started to attract mainstream attention. Advocates say it helps everything from epilepsy to a bad game of tennis, with stops along the way at headaches, insomnia, diminished memory, chronic fatigue syndrome, fibromyalgia, depression, anxiety, chronic pain, obsessive-compulsive disorder, attention deficit disorder, lackluster job performance, and head injury. Although it cannot halt degenerative conditions such as Alzheimer's and Parkinson's, it has been used to alleviate symptoms such as tremors.

---

*The closest anyone comes to you during treatment is to stick electrodes on your head with white paste.*

---

Michael Sitar, a Friendship Heights psychologist, describes neurofeedback training as similar to physical therapy.

"If you've got a weak muscle," he says, "you work to strengthen it. If your brain is under- or overproducing, you work to fix that." Neurofeedback training is, in Sitar's words, "going to the gym to pump neurons."

Consider neurofeedback training a kind of brain gym, except there's no going for the burn. It's not only painless but fun—you play a video game without a joystick or keyboard. You move the images around by thinking.

"What the client is looking at on the computer screen is their brain-wave activity translated into a video game," says Stokes, the Alexandria neurotherapist who treated Jeff.

The closest anyone comes to you during treatment is to stick electrodes on your head with a white paste. These electrodes read the electrical output of your brain's neurons, which form patterns called brain waves. Generally speaking, the slow waves—delta, theta, and alpha—are associated with daydreaming, sleep, or distraction. They're fine if you're meditating or meandering through the woods but can be debilitating if you're trying to finish a task or concentrate.

---

*Flexing brain waves is like weightlifting and seems to have an overall strengthening effect on mental and emotional processes such as mood, anxiety, and cognitive processing.*

---

You need the fast ones, the worker-bee waves—beta and SMR—to get things done. But too many can lead to agitation. It all comes down to balance. Imbalances can be the result of everything from genetics to brain injury to illnesses such as Lyme disease.

A treatment session goes like this: You sit in front of a computer screen with the electrodes pasted to your head reading your brain waves. The brain-training software translates them into video-game images for you to manipulate. In my case it was three rockets chasing an asteroid.

Treatment takes anywhere from 20 to 100 sessions; the average is 50. Over its course, the therapist usually ratchets up the difficulty of the game. That forces your brain to work harder, much like your quadriceps would have to work harder if you added weight to the quad press.

"Neurofeedback mirrors the client's own brain activity back to them in the form of a video game," says Stokes. "The client is asked to change a part of the video game—for instance, to make one rocket ship go faster and one slower. This enables the client to decrease brain-wave amplitudes that may be too strong and increase others that are too weak. Flexing brain waves is like weightlifting and seems to have an overall strengthening effect on mental and emotional processes such as mood, anxiety, and cognitive processing."

While you're playing the video game, the therapist monitors another screen, adjusting the game to make it harder or easier for you to move things around, depending on which brain wave she's trying to adjust.

"Make it go faster," Stokes said to me when I tried it.

"How?" I said.

"Only adults ask that question," she said. "Kids can figure it out."

I channeled my thoughts to the rocket ships, and suddenly they were going faster. When my mind wandered, they went backward. I channeled my concentration and they zoomed forward. When I was finished, I was relaxed and could remember the feeling of zooming myself into concentration.

But my life didn't change dramatically. I went home and promptly lost my keys.

---

*Critics say the research is thin and inconclusive.*

---

Neurofeedback training is nicknamed brain gym for a reason. You can't do one set of leg lifts and expect toned thighs. It took Jeff 15 sessions to notice a difference.

## It's Not Quackery

In the January 2000 editorial in the journal *Clinical Electroen-cephalography*, Frank H. Duffy, a Harvard University professor and pediatric neurologist, wrote of neurofeedback therapy: "In my opinion, if any medication had demonstrated such a wide spectrum of efficacy it would be universally accepted and widely used."

An article in the January 2005 issue of *Child and Adolescent Psychiatric Clinics of North America* said that neurotherapy should be considered "probably efficacious" for the treatment of attention deficit disorder: "Research findings published to date indicate positive clinical response in approximately 75 percent of patients treated in controlled group studies."

Critics say the research is thin and inconclusive. Russell Barkley, a psychiatry professor at the Medical University of South Carolina and founder of the newsletter The ADHD Report, remains skeptical about neurofeedback and attributes gains to a placebo effect.

"Sandra Loo and I reviewed all of the published studies and our conclusion was that the two controlled studies out there found no significant results," he wrote in an e-mail to me. "All other published 'studies' are just uncontrolled presentations of information that lack sufficient scientific rigor to draw any conclusions."

No one, including Barkley, says neurofeedback therapy is harmful. Stokes says she has treated children as young as four years old.

"I generally have been in the closet about neurofeedback with other psychiatrists," says Anderson, the McLean psychiatrist. "Occasionally I'll bring it up and get polite attention, and then the subject quickly changes. They think it's quackery. But I've seen the research, and it's very rewarding because people are getting better."

Anderson has recommended neurofeedback to 40 patients. He says 35 have improved significantly.

EEG stimulation is another form of therapy under the neurotherapy umbrella. Mary Lee Esty, a Chevy Chase neurotherapist, likes EEG because, she says, it works faster than neurofeedback.

"I like to see results quickly," says Esty, who's been using EEG stimulation in her practice since 1994. A colleague told her about it, and she flew to California to observe Len Ochs, the neurotherapist who developed the EEG-stimulation software she uses. She watched him work with patients suffering from brain injury, autism, and fibromyalgia.

"I was blown away by the results," she says. "I knew people like this tend not to get better so quickly. I came back with his software and treated myself. I had no idea how much it would change my ability to remember what I read."

Unlike neurofeedback training, which is noninvasive, EEG stimulation sends a hint of electricity into your brain. One picowatt of power—that's one-trillionth of a watt—pulses through your brain anywhere from two to 30 times a second.

Eight hospital boards have deemed EEG stimulation safe, according to Esty. "A biomedical engineer said that a comparative scale would be powering the lights of Las Vegas on a AAA battery," Esty says. "The stim is so small that most doctors, until they see the effects, believe that it cannot possibly have a therapeutic effect."

The setup is the same as with neurofeedback training: electrodes, white paste, computer. But you don't watch it. You lean back in a recliner, close your eyes, and feel nothing while the computer sends the picowatt of energy your way. It's painless and quick, sometimes lasting less than a minute.

If there were a nanocamera inside your head, it might show this pulsing picowatt of power tickling your brain into producing more endorphins, the body's natural painkillers, and boosting other neurotransmitters like serotonin, which affect mood, body temperature, and sleep, among other things. At least that's the theory.

"It remains to be researched at the cellular level," Esty says. Some doctors, she says, also think that electrical brain stimulation increases blood flow and may stimulate the regrowth of damaged neurons so function can return. But nothing is known for sure yet.

"How many decades did it take to figure out why aspirin worked?" Esty says. "This is a field that needs a lot of research."

That's something everyone—both opponents and proponents—can agree on. The 1998 National Institutes of Health report on ADHD stated that neurotherapy merited further research on the basis of several promising trials.

Esty herself conducted an NIH-funded study, published in the 2001 *Journal of Head Trauma Rehabilitation*, that showed dramatic improvements among brain-injured patients using EEG stimulation.

"None of those people were expected to ever get better," she says. "And we got a bunch of them back to work, not in volunteer jobs but working in their fields."

## A Discordant Brain

For both therapies, the first step is to get what's called a brain map. It's like going to the cardiologist for an electrocardiogram (EKG), except the electrodes are stuck to your head instead of your chest. Like an EKG, the EEG reads electrical output. The therapist can see how your brain is—or is not—working and determine which waves need to be suppressed or increased.

A well-functioning, uninjured brain works with all the waves playing together in concert, says Angelo Bolea, a neuropsychologist and neurofeedback therapist in Bethesda and Annapolis. Imagine an orchestra in which the string instruments drown out the wind section. That's a brain out of whack. Depending on your brain's discord, the consequences range from forgetfulness to cloudy thinking, headaches, depression, even autism.

Brain injury can be caused by a difficult birth, a chronic infection, chemotherapy, or a blow to the head.

Pair an injured brain with the wrong family history and you've got a very troubled kid—like Jeff, the Virginia teen who, according to his mother, inherited mental-health problems on both sides of his family. Plus, when he was four, he ran his bike into a parked car, leaving an egg-shaped bump on his forehead.

Neurofeedback and EEG stimulation are sometimes used together.

---

*In my perfect world, [. . .] the minute a child shows attention disorder or disruptive behavior in school, he or she would get neurofeedback therapy.*

---

"Neurofeedback therapy is the only thing I know of that brings executive functioning back online," says Anderson, the psychiatrist who treated Jeff. By executive functioning, he means prioritizing, sequencing, and shifting thoughts, the necessary tools to navigate through school, work, and life.

Anderson added the therapy to his practice five years ago after a psychologist friend told him about it. "I thought it was a little weird," he says. Then he read the bible of neurofeedback therapy, *A Symphony in the Brain*, by Jim Robbins, went to a neurofeedback conference, and became a believer.

"It all made sense," Anderson says. "There was comprehensive research that overwhelmingly demonstrated the effectiveness of neurofeedback therapy. I thought, this is science. This is not made-up crystal stuff."

He sent his teenage daughter to Stokes, the Alexandria neurofeedback therapist who later treated Jeff, and to Esty, the Chevy Chase neurotherapist who uses EEG stimulation. The results, he says, were remarkable.

"She said it was like her brain suddenly woke up," Anderson says.

## The Walking Wounded

I know the feeling. When the therapists I interviewed for this story would tick off the symptoms of brain injury—fatigue, memory loss, dizziness, intolerance to cold, sensitivity to bright light and noise—I'd say, "Got that, got that, got that." It turned out I was among the walking wounded.

As an infant, I fell off the changing table, head first. That later became a family joke whenever I did something weird. But no one ever made the connection between the fall and my restlessness and disruptive behavior in school.

"In my perfect world," said Esty, "the minute a child shows attention disorder or disruptive behavior in a school, he or she would get neurofeedback therapy."

My head injuries didn't stop with my early fall. As an equestrian, I've had four significant knocks to the head, one requiring ten stitches and another rendering me amnesic for a half hour. There have been several falls that, at the time, didn't seem serious enough to seek medical help.

Muriel Lezak, professor of neurology, psychiatry, and neurological surgery at Oregon Health & Science University, compares the brain to a computer. Imagine, she says, if someone took a hammer and knocked off a few connections here and a few connections there. The programs would run, but some would have a few small errors, slowing down the processing time. The more hits from the hammer, the slower the processing. The destruction of any connection creates a short circuit that has to be bypassed, and as a result, compensatory programs have to be developed, further slowing down processing time. That's your brain after each injury.

I figured I'd had enough blows to the head to cause some kind of damage. But I'd chalked up all the symptoms—forgetfulness, fatigue, inertia, chronic head and neck aches, sensitivity to bright light and cold, brain fog—to the accumulating decades.

I decided to give EEG stimulation a try. The only thing I had to lose was some money. Although EEG stimulation is covered by some insurance companies (for example, Kaiser Permanente), it is not covered by mine. The initial consult for the brain map costs $500. Each session is $90.

I've now had two brain maps—one by Stokes and the other by Esty. Both were revelatory. I was tempted to call my ex-husband and say, "See, I wasn't losing all those library books on purpose like you thought."

No wonder I was tired all the time and it took me forever to get things done—assuming they got done. My theta, delta, and alpha waves had invaded my waking hours, bullying my beta and SMR waves practically off the map. Delta and theta are supposed to be high during sleep or rest. Beta and SMR are the ones that get things done.

Back to the orchestra metaphor: My drums were banging so loud, my violinists had packed up and gone home. My conductor had thrown up his baton in despair and stomped off.

"You're going through life underwater," Esty said. "It's like the heat's on in the house, but it's all escaping through the roof."

She attached two electrodes and hit me with a picowatt of power. I felt nothing.

## No More Lost Keys

For three days, I felt nothing. Still losing things, still inert, still procrastinating. Then on Sunday, I found myself cleaning my car. I'd been thinking about doing that for about a year. After that, I moved all the houseplants back inside for the winter. I'd been thinking about doing that for more than a month. Then came my saddle, bridle, boots, chaps, and anything else leather I could find that hadn't been cleaned in months. I chewed through my entire list of chores that had been rolling around in my head. And come 3 PM, when I'm usually ready for a nap, I was searching for more things to do.

"Wow," was all my husband could say. "You got to keep this brain stuff up."

After my second treatment, when I lectured to my journalism class at Georgetown, I found every word I was looking for. Prior to that, I'd be in the middle of a sentence and forget the word for something as rudimentary as "deadline." I also stopped losing my keys, a minor miracle in my house.

Before EEG stimulation, I'd stop the car, take out the keys, walk in the house, and, without thinking about it, put the keys down someplace. Later, when I went to look for them, I couldn't remember anything after stopping the car.

Now, I'm fully aware of what I'm doing with the keys. Fully aware are the operative words. This may sound like a so-what to anyone who doesn't have this problem. But it was life-changing for me.

I haven't lost my keys in months, and I'm more productive than I've been in years. Most surprisingly, I'm not cold anymore. I actually enjoy winter.

Will it last? Esty says yes. But if I start to slip, I know where I'm heading. Back to the brain-zapper machine.

As for Jeff, things keep getting better for him. In the past, he wrote poems about wanting to die. He recently wrote this:

The boy you hate is finally gone.

He has gone to experience what life never offered

Comfort, love, pleasure without pain and a stress free environment.

Without a rustle of leaves

Or a flutter of wings

He is gone forever.

He is forgotten in the blink of an eye,

Never to be thought of again,

For he is gone.

# Omega-3 Fatty Acids May Help Heal Mental Disorders

*David Servan-Schreiber*

*David Servan-Schreiber is a clinical professor of psychiatry at the University of Pittsburgh. He is also a lecturer in the Faculty of Medicine of Lyon I, in France.*

Patricia was 30 when her second son was born, just a year after her first one. Her partner, Jacques, was proud and happy. Over the previous year with their first child, their domestic life had been a succession of small blessings, and they had deeply desired this second infant. But now Jacques was surprised; Patricia didn't seem very happy. She was even moody and easily upset, taking little interest in the baby, seeking solitude, and sometimes breaking down in tears for no apparent reason. Even the breastfeeding that she had loved with her first baby now felt like a hardship.

Patricia had the "baby blues"—postpartum depression. About 1 young mother out of 10 experiences this condition, which is all the more alarming because it crowds out the happiness commonly anticipated with the birth of a child. The baby was perfect, Jacques's restaurant was increasingly successful—so why was she so unhappy? Neither he nor Patricia could understand this sudden sadness. The doctors tried to reassure them with talk of "hormonal changes" that go along with pregnancy and especially childbirth itself, but that explanation did not really help.

In the last 10 years, an entirely new perspective on Patricia's problem has opened up. She lived in New York, where the daily consumption of one of the most important foods for the brain, the essential "omega-3" fatty acids, is particularly low, just as it is in the United Kingdom, in France, and in Germany. These fatty acids, which the body itself cannot make (hence the term "essential"), play a major role in building the brain and maintaining its balance. That's why these fats are the principal nourishment the fetus takes in through the placenta. And that is also why the mother's reserves, which are already low in our Western-world diets, drop dramatically in the last weeks of pregnancy.

After birth, the omega-3 fatty acids continue to pass through to the baby via the mother's milk, of which they are one of the major components. Breastfeeding thus further depletes the mother's supply for her own body. If a second birth comes in the wake of a first one, as was Patricia's case, and if her diet in the meanwhile has remained poor in fish and shellfish, the principal source of these fatty acids, the mother is at substantial risk of depression.

The "baby blues" occur between three and twenty times more frequently in the United States, France, and Germany than in Japan, Singapore, and Malaysia. According to the *Lancet*, these figures correspond to the differences between the Western and Asian countries with regard to the consumption of fish and shellfish; they can't be attributed simply to the tendency of Asians to hide their symptoms of depression. If Jacques and Patricia had lived in Asia rather than the United States, her second experience of pregnancy and childbirth might have been very different. Understanding why is critical.

## Brain Fuel

The brain is part of the body. Just like all the cells of all other organs, brain cells are continually being renewed. Tomorrow's cells are therefore made up of what we eat today.

One key neurological fact is that two-thirds of the brain is composed of fatty acids. These fats are the basic component of nerve cell membranes, the "envelope" through which all communications with other nerve cells take place, both within the brain and with the rest of the body. The food we eat is directly integrated into these membranes and makes up their substance. If we consume large quantities of saturated fats—such as butter or animal fat, which are solid at room temperature—their rigidity is reflected in the rigidity of the brain cells; if, on the other hand, we take in mostly polyunsaturated fats—those which are liquid at room temperature—the nerve cells' sheaths are more fluid and flexible and communication between them is more stable. Especially when those polyunsaturated fats are omega-3 fatty acids.

The effects of these nutrients on behavior are striking. When omega-3 fatty acids are eliminated from the diet of laboratory rats, the animals' behavior radically changes in a few weeks. They become anxious, stop learning new tasks, and panic in stressful situations, such as seeking an escape route from a water pool. Perhaps even more serious is the fact that a diet low in omega-3 reduces the capacity for pleasure. Much larger doses of morphine are required in these same rats to arouse them, despite the fact that morphine is the very model of easy gratification.

---

*To understand this mysterious effect of omega-3 fatty acids on the brain and emotional balance, it may be necessary to go back to the origins of humanity.*

---

On the other hand, a team of European researchers has shown that a diet rich in omega-3—such as the Eskimo's, consisting of up to 16 grams a day of fish oil—leads, in the long run, to the increased production of neurotransmitters for energy and positive mood in the emotional brain.

## Happier and Smarter with Omega-3

The fetus and the newborn child, with their rapidly developing brains, have the greatest need for omega-3 fatty acids. A recent Danish study published in the *British Medical Journal* shows that women who take in more omega-3 in their everyday diet during pregnancy have heavier and healthier infants, as well as fewer premature births. Another Danish study, published this time in the *Journal of the American Medical Association*, demonstrates that children who were breastfed for at least 9 months and who also received a great quantity of omega-3 in their diet have a higher IQ than others 20 or 30 years later. And women in countries with the highest consumption of fish and the highest omega-3 levels in their breast milk are also considerably less likely to suffer from postpartum depression. But the role of omega-3 is by no means limited to pregnancy. . . .

## The First Diet of *Homo Sapiens*

To understand this mysterious effect of omega-3 fatty acids on the brain and emotional balance, it may be necessary to go back to the origins of humanity. There are two types of "essential fatty acids": omega-3s and omega-6s. Omega-3s come from algae, plankton, and some leaves, including grass. Omega-6s come primarily from grains and abound in most vegetable oils and in animal fat, especially in the meat of animals fed with grains. Though omega-6s are also important constituents of cells, when present in excess they provoke inflammation responses throughout the body that can lead to a multitude of problems (we will return to this below).

---

*Today, the consumption of omega-3 fatty acids in the Western diet may be less than half what it was before World War II.*

---

At the time when the modern human brain developed, the early humanoids lived around the lakes of the Great Rift in East Africa. Scientists now believe that their food supply was perfectly balanced, with a ratio of 1-to-1 of omega-3s and omega-6s. This ideal ratio would have provided their bodies with the perfect building blocks for new kinds of neurons that developed new abilities such as self-consciousness, language, and the usage of tools.

Today, the widespread development of certain livestock industry practices, including feeding livestock with grain rather than grass, in addition to the presence of omega-6-rich vegetable oil in all types of processed foods, has created a marked imbalance between omega-6s and omega-3s. The typical ratio of 3s to 6s in the Western diet is 1-to-10 to 1-to-20. Some nutritionists have described our brains today as sophisticated race car engines meant to run on highly refined fuel that are instead asked to putter along on diesel.

That mismatch between what the brain needs and what we feed it in America and in Europe would explain, in part, the large differences in the rates of depression between Western and Asian countries. In places such as Taiwan, Hong Kong, or Japan—where fish and seafood consumption is the highest—the rates of depression are considerably lower than in the United States. This remains true even after taking into account cultural differences that may effect self-disclosure of depressive symptoms. The mismatch may have also contributed to the rapid growth of depression in the West over the last 50 years. Today, the consumption of omega-3 fatty acids in the Western diet may be less than half of what it was before World War II. And it is precisely since that period that rates of depression have risen considerably.

An excess of omega-6s in the body leads to inflammation reactions. One of the more striking developments in recent medical research is the revelation that all of the leading illnesses in the Western world are caused or worsened by inflammatory reactions: cardiovascular diseases—such as coronary artery disease, myocardial infarctions, or strokes—but also cancer, arthritis, and even Alzheimer's disease. And there is a striking overlap between countries with the highest rates of cardiovascular diseases and those with the highest rates of depression. This does, indeed, suggest the possibility of common causes for both. And, in fact, omega-3s have well-established benefits for cardiac diseases, known for a much longer time than those that have just been studied with respect to depression. . . .

## Is Depression Inflammation?

The discovery of the important role of omega-3 fatty acids in the prevention and treatment of depression raises entirely new questions about the nature of this disorder. What if depression were an inflammatory disease, as we now know is the case for coronary artery disease, the leading cause of death in Western societies? An inflammation theory of depression may begin to explain a number of puzzling observations about this disease that most contemporary theories—entirely focused on neurotransmitters such as serotonin—have been dutifully ignoring.

---

*In the end, Tibetan medicine may be right: Depression is perhaps as much a physical illness as it is a disorder of the mind.*

---

Take the situation of Nancy, for example. She was 65 when she experienced her first episode of depression. Nothing had changed in her life, and she just could not understand why she would suddenly become depressed. Yet, her family doctor pointed out that she had symptoms of sadness and hopelessness, lack of energy, fatigue, impaired concentration, no appetite, and even weight loss. All of these were, he insisted, typical symptoms of depression and met the diagnostic criteria for major depressive disorder of the American Psychiatric Association.

Six months later, before she had even agreed to start treatment for her depression, Nancy noticed a persistent pain in her stomach. The ultrasound that her doctor ordered revealed a large tumor on the edge of her liver. Nancy had pancreatic cancer. As is often the case in this illness, her cancer had manifested first with a depression rather than with physical symptoms. Several types of cancer induce widespread inflammatory reactions well before the tumor becomes large enough for detection. That inflammatory state, which is sometimes subtle, may well be responsible for the symptoms of depression that precede the diagnosis of cancer. In fact, depression is common in all physical illnesses that have a diffuse inflammatory component, such as infections (pneumonia, the flu, typhoid fever), cerebrovascular accidents ("strokes"), myocardial infarctions, and autoimmune disorders. I wonder, therefore, to what extent "classic" depressions may also be caused by inflammatory processes. That would not be much of a surprise, since we know that stress in and of itself causes inflammatory reactions—which is the reason why it also worsens acne, arthritis, and most autoimmune diseases. Since a long period of stress often precedes depression, it may well be that depressive symptoms are caused directly by stress-related inflammation. In the end, Tibetan medicine may be right: Depression is perhaps as much a physical illness as it is a disorder of the mind.

## Where Can You Find Omega-3 Essential Fatty Acids?

The primary sources of omega-3 fatty acids are algae and plankton. These find their way to our kitchens and plates through fish and seafood that accumulate the fatty acids in their fat tissue. Cold water fish—richer in fat—are therefore the best sources of omega-3s. Farm-raised fish may be less rich in omega-3s than fish from the wild. Ocean-fished salmon, for example, is an excellent source of omega-3s, but farm-raised salmon is not as reliable.

The most reliable sources of omega-3s, and the least contaminated by mercury, dioxin, and organic carcinogens, are the smaller fish, because they're found at the bottom of the food chain. These are mackerel (one of the richest sources of omega-3s), anchovies (whole, not the small salted fillets found on pizza), sardines, and herring. Other good fish sources of omega-3s are tuna, haddock, and trout. . . .

Good vegetarian sources of omega-3s also exist, though they require one more step in metabolism to become actual constituents of neural membranes. These are flax seeds (which can be eaten as such, ground, or slightly roasted), flaxseed oil, canola (rapeseed) oil, hemp oil, and English walnuts. All green leafy vegetables contain precursors of omega-3 fatty acids, though in lesser amounts. One of the best vegetable sources is purslane (a basic staple of Roman cooking 2,000 years ago, and still commonly used in modern Greece). Omega-3s can also be derived from spinach, seaweeds, and spirulina (a traditional part of the Aztec diet).

The meat of wild or farm animals that feed on grass and natural leaves also contains omega-3s. For this reason, wild game is generally much richer in omega-3s than livestock (at least nonorganic livestock). The more grain livestock is fed, the lower the omega-3 content of its flesh. A report published in the *New England Journal of Medicine* shows, for example, that the eggs of free-range chickens contain 20 times more omega-3s than those of grain-fed hens. The meat of grain-fed livestock also becomes richer in omega-6s, with their *pro-inflammatory* properties. Therefore, in order to maintain a balance between omega-3s and omega-6s, it is important to limit meat consumption to a maximum of three servings per week, and to avoid fatty meats, even those richer in omega-6s, and saturated fats that compete with omega-3s.

All vegetable oils are rich in omega-6s and none contain omega-3s, except flaxseed oil, canola (rapeseed) oil, and hemp oil, each of which is at least one-third omega-3. (Flaxseed oil is more than 50 percent omega-3s, making it the best vegetable source of these essential fatty acids.) Olive oil can be used freely; it does not contain many omega-3s or omega-6s, so it does not affect the ratio. To approach an omega-3-to-omega-6 ratio as close as possible to 1-to-1, you should aim to eliminate almost all the usual cooking oils, except for olive oil and canola (rapeseed) oil. Avoiding frying oil is particularly important; in addition to its omega-6 content, frying oil has many free radicals that produce oxidative reactions inside the body.

Butter, cream, and full-fat dairy products should be eaten with moderation because they compete with omega-3s for integration within cells. Yet, Serge Renaud, who conducted research on cheese and yogurt in France, has demonstrated that these products—even made from whole milk—are much less toxic than other milk products because their high calcium and magnesium content reduces the absorption of saturated fats. This is the reason why Artemis Simopoulos, M.D., former chair of the Nutrition Coordinating Committee at the National Institutes of Health, considers that up to 30 grams of cheese per day are acceptable in her "Omega Diet Plan." In addition, some new and intriguing studies suggest that dairy products, eggs, and even meat derived from animals fed in part with flax seeds—about 5 percent of the animals' diet—may help reduce cholesterol as well as insulin resistance in type 2 diabetes. These products may become a very important source of omega-3s in the future.

## What Is the Best Dose of Omega-3?

The findings from existing studies suggest that in order to obtain an antidepressant effect, one must consume between 1 and 10 grams per day of the combination of DHA (docosahexaenoic acid) and EPA (eicosapentaenoic acid)—the two forms of omega-3s commonly found in fish oil. In practice, many people opt for an omega-3 supplement in order to be sure they're receiving a sufficiently pure, reliable, and quality "dosage" of the nutrient. Several products are available from supplement manufacturers, in the form of either capsules or oil. The best products are probably those that have the highest concentration of EPA with respect to DHA. Some authors, such as Dr. Stoll and David Horrobin, M.D., Ph.D., former chair of medicine at the University of Montreal, suggest that it is mostly EPA that has an antidepressant effect and that too much DHA may actually block the effect, requiring higher doses of the combined oil than if the product is more concentrated in EPA. Indeed, a study from the Baylor College of Medicine found that a pure DHA supplement had no effect against depression, which contrasts sharply with the results of studies using EPA. Products with a very high EPA concentration (at least seven times more EPA than DHA) may require only 1 gram per day of EPA. This is the dose that was used in three studies that looked specifically at patients with depressive symptoms.

---

*Despite the fact that some patients balk at the idea of taking "fat" supplements, omega-3 based-oils do not seem to make people gain weight.*

---

Products that contain a bit of vitamin E are better protected against oxidation, which may render the oil ineffective or even, in rare cases, toxic. Some doctors recommend combining an omega-3 supplement with a daily vitamin supplement that contains vitamin E (no more than 800 Internationl Units per day), vitamin C (no more than 1,000 milligrams per day), and selenuim (no more than 200 *micro*grams per day) to prevent oxidation of the omega-3 fatty acids inside the body. However, I did not find any evidence that this extensive supplementary regimen was truly necessary.

Cod liver oil, a favorite of our grandparents as a source of vitamin A and D, is not a reliable long-term source of omega-3 fatty acids. Taking an adequate dose of cod liver oil for depression would require such large amounts that it might result in a dangerous overload of vitamin A.

Curiously, despite the fact that some patients balk at the idea of taking "fat" supplements, omega-3-based oils do not seem to make people gain weight. In his study of patients with bipolar illness, Dr. Stoll noted that patients did not gain weight in spite of their daily intake of 9 grams of fish oil. In fact, some even lost weight. In a study performed with mice, those who were fed a diet particularly rich in omega-3s were 25 percent leaner than those who ate exactly the same amount of calories, but without omega-3s. Some authors have suggested that the way the body metabolizes omega-3s reduces the buildup of fat tissue.

The only side effects from omega-3 supplements are fishy aftertaste (usually eliminated by taking the supplements in divided doses at the beginning of meals); occasional loose stools or mild diarrhea (which may require reducing the dose for a few days); and, in rare cases, bruising or increased bleeding time. People who are taking anticoagulant medicines such as Coumadin, or even a daily aspirin (which also increases bleeding time), should be careful not to take more than 1,000 milligrams per day of fish oil, and to consult their physician.

## The Judgment of History

On the day historians begin to analyze the history of medicine in the 20th century, I believe they will point out two major events. The first one, without any doubt, was the discovery of antibiotics, which practically eradicated bacterial pneumonia—the leading cause of death in the West until World War II. The second is a revolution that is still in the making: the scientific demonstration that nutrition has a profound impact on practically all the leading causes of disease in Western societies.

Cardiologists and internists have been the first to integrate this fundamental idea into their practices (even if, to this day, they rarely recommend omega-3 diets or supplements, despite the large number of studies published in respected journals that have documented their effects, as well as the explicit recommendations of the American Heart Association). Most psychiatrists lag far behind. Yet the brain is almost certainly as sensitive to the contents of our daily diets as the heart may be. When we regularly intoxicate our brain with alcohol or street drugs, it suffers. When we fail to nourish it with the nutrients it needs, it suffers, too. What's truly astonishing is that it's taken so long for modern Western science to come back to this very basic realization. All traditional medicines, whether Tibetan, Chinese, Ayurvedic, or Greco-Roman, have emphasized the importance of nutrition since their earliest texts. Hippocrates wrote: "Let your food be your treatment, and your treatment your food." That was 2,400 years ago.

# CHAPTER 4

# How Should Society Respond to the Mentally Ill?

# Chapter Preface

Society's view of mental illness has come a long way since the first half of the twentieth century when the mentally ill were stigmatized and could be sent away to endure harsh prison-like conditions with no hope for a cure. They might be exposed to such cruelties as bloodletting, ice-water baths, and primitive electroshock treatment. Robert Whitaker, author of *Mad in America: Bad Science, Bad Medicine, and the Enduring Mistreatment of the Mentally Ill*, writes that mental asylums in the United States were historically run as "facilities that served to segregate the misfits from society rather than as hospitals that provided medical care." Unless forced sterilizations and lobotomies are counted as medical care; thousands of those procedures were performed. The mentally ill were not even allowed to wed for support; as late as 1933, there were no states in which the insane could legally marry.

It is no wonder people tried to hide their problems with mental health. Today it is different. Mental illness is far less stigmatized. People talk about their mental health struggles on the *Oprah Winfrey Show*, and mental health issues have percolated into the realm of sitcoms. Miranda, a character in the HBO series *Sex and the City*, suffers a panic attack in the second season of the show when she is struggling with singledom and buying her first New York City apartment. The character Tony Soprano in the HBO drama series *The Sopranos* regularly sees a therapist, and in season three he is even reassured by the mob boss Carmine Lupertazzi that seeing a therapist is nothing to be ashamed of: "There's no stigma," says the boss.

Critics of this trend say that publicizing so-called "milder" mental illnesses does not do a lot for people suffering from severe mental illnesses, and in fact may further push these people into the margins of society. In 1999, Andrew Goldstein, the man who killed a woman named Kendra Webdale by shoving her into the path of a New York City subway train, is said to have repeatedly sought medication for his condition (schizophrenia), but he just couldn't get it. In the current bean-counting era of managed care, society is erring on the side of neglect, critics say, whereas the early years of U.S. mental health erred more on the side of more overt forms of cruelty.

Cultural phenomena such as Ken Kesey's novel *One Flew over the Cuckoo's Nest*, which depicted the jailers as crazier than the inmates, have also played a role in shaping today's views on mental illness. Society has responded to such influences over time by taking more of a hands-off approach, arguing that the mentally ill should be free to make decisions about their treatments without treatments or medication being forced on them. Critics of this approach say that people who are mentally ill often don't realize they are ill, and the concept of involuntary commitment—the enforcement of treatment and/or medication—can ultimately free the mentally ill from the bonds of their disease.

The concept of screening tests for teen mental illness is another area where the issue of control is significant, with advocates saying that such screening tests are lifesavers, while critics say the tests lack the complex approach needed to truly diagnose a mental illness, but instead violate privacy and are the result of pharmaceutical company over-involvement, and can end up stigmatizing teens and their families. Another controversial area examined in this chapter is the legal response to mental illness. Social critics are angry that the insanity defense fails to hold people accountable for their actions, while mental health advocates argue that the mentally ill should receive treatment, not punishment. There are no easy answers to the controversies explored in this chapter.

# The Stigma of Mental Illness Must Be Overcome

*Kay Redfield Jamison*

*Kay Redfield Jamison is a professor of psychiatry and writer who is one of the foremost experts on bipolar disorder (also known as manic depression). She has been named one of the "Best Doctors in the United States" and was chosen by* Time *magazine as a "Hero of Medicine."*

Much of the stigma of mental illness is engrained in deep and ancient attitudes held by virtually every society on earth. These attitudes govern the decisions societies make and the behaviours they tolerate. Newspapers and television stations can print or broadcast statements about those with mental illness that simply would not be tolerated if they were said about any other minority group. Stigma also insinuates itself into policy decisions, access to care, health insurance, employment discrimination, and in research allocations and priorities. Unfortunately, people who have mental illness also stigmatise themselves. They make few demands and their expectations are frighteningly low—with grave consequences. Stigma can kill.

The inability to discuss mental illness in an informed and straightforward way, to deal with it as the major public health concern that it is, is unjustifiable. There is a very large group that I think of as the silent successful—people who get well from psychiatric illness but who are afraid to speak out. This reluctance is very understandable, very human, but it is unfortunate because it perpetuates the misperception that mental illness cannot be treated. What remains visible in the public eye are the newspaper accounts of violence, the homeless mentally ill, the untreated illness in friends, family, and col-

Kay Redfield Jamison, "The Many Stigmas of Mental Illness," *The Lancet*, February 11, 2006. Reproduced by permission.

leagues. What is not seen are all the truck drivers, secretaries, teachers, lawyers, physicians, and government officials who have been successfully treated, who work, compete, and succeed.

## Solving the Mystery of Stigma

My own perspective on stigma is shaped not only by being a professional who studies mental illness but as someone who has suffered from manic depression since I was 16 years old. I strongly believe that we need to better understand why stigma exists, and not just from a sociological or anthropological point of view. Studies of animal behaviour make it very clear that animals discriminate not only against those who are markedly odd, but also against those who are different in more subtle ways. I believe that the expression of stigma or discrimination is deep-wired into the brain. There are good reasons for fear, which have to do with the unknown, the unpredictable, and the potentially violent. We have to acknowledge upfront that untreated mental illnesses can be frightening and that it can be associated with violent acts. Indeed, we know from many studies that 50% of manic episodes are characterised by at least one act of physical violence. We also know that moods are contagious. Hypomania and depression can spread across members of a group like wildfire. That is, in part, what moods are for—to affect others in a group. So we have to acknowledge that mental illness can have a powerful effect on those close to it.

Second, I believe that research is the greatest destigmatiser. We need to get people interested in the brain, and in the fact that these are very interesting illnesses. We need to capture the imaginations of the young and explain that understanding the brain is the last great frontier. To make an illness interesting is to some extent to help destigmatise it.

Third, we need to start within our own clinical community and have more honest and open discussions about impaired doctors, psychologists, and nurses. Unless we are willing to talk about how to deal with mental illness among professionals the problem is going to remain undiscussed, creating more fear and more stigmatisation. We also need to standardise the teaching of the clinical science underlying these illnesses. Some of the stigma associated with mental illness exists because there has been so much bad teaching and inadequate treatment over the years.

We also need to recognise that those of us who have mental illnesses represent a very large block of voters. If you look at the numbers, we have not advocated well. We have not used the political power we have. We need better public awareness campaigns. Public perception about mental illness lags decades behind the science. We need to convey how real and extensive our scientific understanding is, the effectiveness of existing treatments, and the promise research holds for the future.

The stigma that those with psychiatric illness face is only truly understood by those who have been on the receiving end of it. This became more painfully clear to me when I wrote a book, *An Unquiet Mind*, that recounted my own experience with manic-depressive illness.

I received thousands of letters from people. Most of them were supportive but many were exceedingly hostile. A striking number said that I deserved my illness because I was insufficiently Christian and that the devil had gotten hold of me. More prayer, not medication, was the only answer. Others were irate that I had continued my professional work, even though my illness was well-controlled. The most upsetting letters, however, were from doctors, psychologists, and nurses who wrote about their own mood disorders, suicide attempts, and substance misuse problems. All made the irrefutable point that it was disingenuous for hospitals and medical schools to expect health-care professionals to be straightforward about mental illness when their hospital privileges, referral sources, and licences to practice were on the line. This is undeniably true.

The chairmen of my academic departments have been compassionate and supportive of my career. I am fortunate in this regard; most others in my situation are not. Mental illness is as least as common in our colleagues as it is in the general public, which is to say it is common. Suicide occurs far too often. We need to reach out to our colleagues. As mentors and educators we need to be proactive, we need to educate medical students, house staff, and graduate students about depression and other mental illnesses. We need to make it easy for them to get treatment. We need as well to educate them more effectively about how best to diagnose and treat mental illness in their patients. We as a profession also need to reach out to society to say that we will not tolerate the kind of pain and discrimination that has gone on for far too long.

When I wrote my book I had no idea what the long-term consequences of being public about my manic-depressive illness would be. I assumed that they were bound to be better than continuing to be silent. I was tired of hiding and tired of the hypocrisy. I was tired of being held hostage to stigma and tired of perpetuating it. Now there is indeed no turning back and I find myself continuing to take solace in [poet] Robert Lowell's question, the one which had been at the heart of my decision to be public about my illness: "Yet why not say what happened?"

# Involuntary Commitment Is Essential

*John Pekkanen*

*John Pekkanen is a writer who covers medical issues. He is the author of several books.*

It was a mild day, the beginning of spring break in the Alexandria schools. Eight-year-old Kevin Shifflett was playing in front of his great-grandmother's house, a brick duplex in the Del Ray neighborhood of Alexandria. Kevin was using a twig to dig out dirt between cracks in the sidewalk.

A few minutes before 4 o'clock, a stranger walked up. Police later described him as a black man, medium height and build, possibly wearing a long-sleeve crew-neck sweater. Grabbing Kevin from behind, he slashed at the boy with a knife.

Kevin's 11-year-old sister, Katie, ran screaming into the house. Thelma Taylor, 81, the boy's great-grandmother, ran outside and grabbed at the assailant. The man struck her hard with the butt end of his knife and stabbed a 51-year-old woman who tried to help. Then he ran away.

Kevin, who had been stabbed 18 times, was pronounced dead at the scene.

The murder of Kevin Shifflett on April 19, 2000, was front-page news. It was shocking. People searched for answers, found none, and concluded it was one of those random incidents that could not have been predicted or prevented.

' The opposite is much closer to the truth. The murder was almost predictable and almost certainly preventable.

## Strange Behavior Was Overlooked

The warning signs that Kevin's accused killer, Gregory D. Murphy, 30, was dangerous, violent, and mentally disturbed were impossible to miss. Murphy, who grew up in Alexandria as the

John Pekkanen, "Dangerous Minds," *Washingtonian*, July 2002. Reproduced by permission of the author.

youngest of two sons of David and Edna Mae Murphy, struggled in elementary school and repeated the third grade. At 15, he was accused of shooting and wounding another teenager. In court, he was ordered to undergo a psychological examination.

At 16, he began treatment for mental illness. The treatment ended within a few months, apparently because Murphy didn't show up for appointments, according to court records.

Over the next few years, Murphy established a criminal record that included arrests for assault, cocaine possession with intent to sell, and petty larceny. He was twice charged with rape but never prosecuted.

During one stint in the Fairfax Adult Detention Center, Murphy struck another inmate without provocation. At a hearing, Murphy, who is black, swore at the judge, who is white, and called him a racist.

---

*Over the past three decades, political, legal, and social forces have joined to bring about the virtual collapse of this country's system of mental-health care.*

---

In 1993, Murphy was arrested and convicted for the malicious wounding of a stranger at a Virginia filling station. He had struck the man repeatedly with a hammer.

Imprisoned at the Augusta Correctional Center in western Virginia, Murphy displayed textbook signs of severe mental illness. He complained to authorities that "high level people" throughout Virginia, Maryland, and the District—including the FBI—had tried to kill him "numerous times."

On one occasion, Murphy said he was insane and tortured by the prison staff—and had "the paperwork" to prove it. Later, he said, "I have never been paranoid a day in my life."

Murphy's behavior seemed to stir little but passing interest. One prison guard reported he was "acting strange lately"; another noted he was "being suspicious and paranoid." He was seen by a social worker and psychiatrist, but he refused medication. He underwent a 72-hour stay on the mental-health unit for observation but received no treatment, according to court records.

On April 7, 2000, Murphy was released on mandatory parole, as required by Virginia. If authorities didn't know they were putting someone on the street who posed a threat to the community, they should have. Though no formula perfectly predicts whether a mentally ill person will become violent, anyone with a history of violence, substance abuse, and untreated psychosis is a prime candidate.

Murphy walked out of prison and back into society. Twelve days after his release, police say, he attacked Kevin Shifflett. After his arrest for the murder, Murphy was at last evaluated by psychiatrists. The diagnosis: paranoid schizophrenia.

In April of this year, Tammy and Art Shifflett, Kevin's parents, filed a wrongful-death lawsuit that blamed state prison officials for making the murder of their son possible. They charged that Murphy, despite obvious signs of mental instability while in prison, was never evaluated or treated. Upon his release, they claimed, Murphy's parole officer ignored orders of the state parole board to monitor him electronically.

In June, the Shiffletts withdrew their lawsuit when it was discovered that the parole board had not required electronic monitoring of Murphy. But the family still believes authorities are to blame.

---

*At a time when new and better drugs offer severely mentally ill people a chance to lead more normal and productive lives, only half are effectively treated.*

---

"There were a series of breakdowns all along the way that allowed Murphy to be out on the street," says Blair Brown, the Shiffletts' lawyer. "At the very least, the state should have sought a court order to place Murphy in a mental-health facility to diagnose and possibly treat him. He would have fought it, but he would have lost."

## In Harm's Way?

Over the past three decades, political, legal, and social forces have joined to bring about the virtual collapse of this country's system of mental-health care. You can see this on the streets, which are home to thousands of people with severe mental illness. And you can see it in the jails, which by default have become the country's chief caretaker of the mentally ill.

With good intentions, laws were passed to protect the rights of the mentally ill. But the same laws leave families, medical professionals, and judges little legal leverage to mandate treatment. Even the mentally ill who are too sick to understand they are sick cannot be forced to get treatment.

The result? At a time when new and better drugs offer severely mentally ill people a chance to lead more normal and productive lives, only half are effectively treated. And people with severe mental illness and a history of violence—people like Gregory Murphy—are routinely allowed to move among us untreated and unmonitored.

"I'd like to say that the circumstances leading to the murder of Kevin Shifflett were unusual," says Dr. E. Fuller Torrey, director of the Bethesda-based Stanley Foundation Research Programs, which give out grants for study of psychiatric diseases. "But they're not. Things like this routinely happen every day in this country."

People with a history of severe mental illness commit about 1,000 murders each year, according to the Treatment Advocacy Center, an Arlington nonprofit that seeks to eliminate barriers to treatment. That estimate, which is based on US Justice Department statistics, is thought to be conservative.

Gregory Murphy's case is reminiscent of the 1998 shooting at the US Capitol. Russell Weston Jr. stands accused of blasting his way into the building with a .38-caliber revolver and killing two police officers, Jacob Chestnut and John Gibson, and wounding a third, Douglas McMillan.

Like Murphy, Weston has a history of mental illness, violence, and nontreatment. He came to Washington in search of a "ruby-red satellite" that he believed would turn back time and "save the world from cannibals." Law-enforcement and mental-health officials knew of Weston's mental instability.

## The Odds of Violence

According to the National Institute of Mental Health, more than 4 million Americans suffer from bipolar disorder (manic depression) or schizophrenia, the two most severe forms of mental illness.

Symptoms of bipolar disorder—such as sharp mood swings and delusional behavior—usually develop in late adolescence or early adulthood. Men typically show signs of schizophrenia—visual and/or auditory hallucinations, disordered and sometimes paranoid thinking—at about that age, but women generally develop symptoms later—in their late twenties and early thirties.

Advances in antipsychotics, mood stabilizers, and antidepressants allow many with these diseases to lead more normal lives. Medication improves up to three-quarters of schizophrenic patients and even more people with bipolar disorder.

*Studies have made clear that severely mentally ill people who take their medication are no more violent than people in the general population.*

Drug therapy helps order thinking and diminish delusions and hallucinations. Sometimes it lends the sick enough insight to realize they are ill and need continuing treatment.

Research strongly suggests that severe mental illness, like many diseases, is most effectively controlled when treated early. One study of 82 schizophrenic patients found that delays in treatment worsened the illness. Untreated psychotic episodes work cumulatively to diminish mental capacity and deepen delusions and hallucinations. Delays in treatment also increase the chances of damage to cognitive function.

The seriously mentally ill who go untreated are more violent than the general population. A 1992 study in the American Sociological Review found that people with severe mental illness were three times more likely than others to commit serious violence. The sicker the person, the study concluded, the greater the potential for violence.

Today, the percentage of seriously mentally ill people in prison is nearly six times that found in the general population. The suicide rate among the mentally ill is 10 to 15 times higher.

Research indicates that violent behavior can be curbed through drug therapy. In a 1997 study of 348 severely ill mental patients in custody in Virginia, those who refused medication were more likely to get into fights and to require seclusion than medicated patients were.

Similarly, a 1998 study by the MacArthur Foundation concluded that individuals with severe mental illness committed twice as many acts of violence immediately before being hospitalized as they did after their release, when they were taking medication.

Says Mary Zdanowicz, executive director of the Treatment Advocacy Center, "Studies have made clear that severely mentally ill people who take their medication are no more violent than people in the general population."

## Without Meds For Severe Illness, Everyone Loses

Russell Weston was not good about taking his medicine. According to interviews his family gave after the Capitol shooting, Weston began acting delusional in his early twenties, just after graduating from high school in Valmeyer, a small Illinois town bordering the Mississippi River.

A few years later, he was diagnosed as a paranoid schizophrenic. Weston fantasized that he worked for the CIA or Secret Service and was being hunted by snipers and Navy Seals. The government, he told his parents, sent him messages through fillings in his teeth.

In the fall of 1996, Weston threatened President Clinton, who he believed planned to drop an atomic bomb on his house. At the request of the Secret Service, he was evaluated at an Illinois mental facility. He refused treatment.

---

*Studies have found that at least 40 percent of those who suffer from severe mental illness don't believe they are ill.*

---

Later, while living in Montana, Weston went to a local hospital for what his parents say was an allergy or infection. But his delusions surfaced—he accused a lab technician of trying to poison him while drawing his blood—and Weston was committed to a state mental institution.

Early in his stay, he tried to punch a nurse. But he improved under drug therapy. After 53 days, doctors released him and told him to continue taking his medication.

Returning to Illinois, Weston visited a local mental-health center but learned that no further treatment had been mandated. His family told reporters he took his medication for a few days but refused their pleas to continue. "What are we going to do with a 41-year-old man?" said Arbah Weston, his mother. "You can't throw him in the car and drive him to the doctor."

Many families of the mentally ill voice similar frustrations. In a comfortable Montgomery County home, parents told the story of their son, a brilliant student who became delusional and irrational toward the end of college. After graduating, he disappeared. His parents tracked him down hundreds of miles from home, living in a car, a captive of his own delusions.

They were able to commit him to a mental hospital, but his stay was too brief to do any lasting good.

For several years their son, who has never been violent, refused medication. Though a schizophrenic, he insisted—and continues to insist—he's not sick. That's not unusual. Studies have found that at least 40 percent of those who suffer from severe mental illness don't believe they are ill. This stems from more than denial. It is the result of a brain condition called anosognosia, which may be caused by organic damage to the frontal lobe, the area of the brain that acts as an executive manager.

The parents finally used a trick to coerce their son into taking medication. He takes it regularly now, and he is no longer delusional. Ultimately, the son's schizophrenia went untreated for ten years. The couple believes it did irreparable damage to his IQ and his emotional balance.

"He lost so much all those years he didn't take medication," his mother says. "If we could have treated him earlier, I'm convinced he'd be so much better now."

## Deciding Their Own Care

These parents learned a hard truth: It is virtually impossible today to impose psychiatric treatment. Legally, even the seriously mentally ill who have no idea they are sick have virtually complete control over their care.

The laws that define this power took root in the 1950s and '60s. One key event was the 1948 publication of *The Shame of States*, a book that described the deplorable conditions of many mental hospitals. At the time, state mental-health facilities held more than 500,000 patients.

The book, as well as news stories, exposed beatings and other cruel treatment in these hospitals, which were often poorly run and unsanitary. Many patients were warehoused for life with virtually no legal recourse.

The early 1950s also saw the introduction of the first effective antipsychotic drugs—Thorazine for schizophrenia and lithium for bipolar disorder—which proved mental illnesses could be treated.

By the 1960s, an antipsychiatry movement was under way that still has influence. Scottish psychiatrist R.D. Laing emerged as a college-campus cult hero for his books *The Divided Self* and *The Politics of Experience*, in which he argued that schizophrenia was a "special strategy" invented by people to cope with stresses in life. Laing, who later recanted many of his views, also claimed that schizophrenia was not a "condition" but a "voyage into inner space."

The other founding father of the antipsychiatry movement was Thomas Szasz, a New York psychoanalyst. His book *The Myth of Mental Illness* denied the very existence of mental illness—a view Szasz and others still hold today. According to Szasz, we label as mentally ill those who may be bothersome or different. Szasz wrote that calling someone mentally ill makes "more palatable the bitter pill of moral conflicts in human relations."

Laing and Szasz lent intellectual respectability to demands by the New Left in the 1960s and '70s to "liberate" the mentally ill from mental hospitals and psychiatrists. Psychiatry, it claimed, was an instrument of oppression.

The antipsychiatry movement made its way into popular culture. The message of movies such as *One Flew over the Cuckoo's Nest* and *The King of Hearts* was plain: The inmates weren't crazy, their keepers were.

The new political and social attitudes led to changes in laws concerning the rights of the mentally ill. Class-action lawsuits rolled back the legal instruments by which individuals were committed to mental institutions. Family members, psychiatrists, and mental-health officials were stripped of power to make treatment-related decisions on behalf of the seriously mentally ill. That power was given almost exclusively to the sick—no matter how debilitating their illness.

Under the new laws, involuntary commitment was permitted only in cases of "proven dangerousness." Judges generally interpret this standard strictly and make it difficult to meet. They conclude danger must be "imminent" or "current" to order involuntary treatment.

In most cases, the courts interpret "dangerousness" to imply a physical threat. Verbal abuse is generally not considered. Also, if authorities don't witness violent behavior or have direct evidence of it, there is often little they can do. Many parents admit that they hope their mentally ill son or daughter will act in a violent way that won't hurt anyone but will lead to hospitalization and treatment.

"Under these laws, the seriously mentally ill who refuse treatment because they don't think there is anything wrong with them are allowed to become as miserable and as sick as they want," says the Stanley Foundation's Torrey, whose younger sister has schizophrenia and doesn't acknowledge it. "If you want a definition of insanity, that's it."

Ironically, what's been done to "free" the mentally ill from oppression often imprisons them in their disease. "All these civil-liberties laws were passed in the name of freedom and autonomy for the mentally ill," says Dr. Sally Satel, a psychiatrist, author, and fellow at the American Enterprise Institute. "But what was overlooked then and now was the fact that there is no freedom in psychosis. It limits freedom. The whole point of treatment, even if it has to be forcible at times, is to reduce the risk of violence and enhance the personal autonomy of the mentally ill."

# Involuntary Commitment Is Unconstitutional

## Beth Haroules

*Beth Haroules is a staff attorney at the New York Civil Liberties Union.*

My name is Beth Haroules. I am a Staff Attorney at the New York Civil Liberties Union (NYCLU). The NYCLU is the New York affiliate of the American Civil Liberties Union and has long been devoted to the protection and enhancement of those fundamental rights and constitutional values embodied in the Bill of Rights and in the New York State Constitution. Those rights include the rights of personal liberty and bodily integrity deeply implicated by this controversy. We thank you for the opportunity to testify before you this morning.

In 1999, with the adoption of "Kendra's Law," the New York State Legislature expanded the circumstance under which the State may compel persons with psychiatric disabilities to undergo treatment against his or her will or to participate involuntarily in mental health programs even if those individuals do not meet the criteria for involuntary hospitalization and/or medication.

The right of a person to determine his or her course of medical treatment has long been recognized as a fundamental right by the courts in this country. In *Matter [v.] Storer* the New York Court of Appeals recognized that a patient's right to choose his own medical treatment was superior to the doctor's obligation to provide care, even if the medical treatment was necessary to preserve the patient's life. And, in the seminal

Beth Haroules, "Statement of Beth Haroules Before the Assembly Standing Committee on Mental Health, Mental Retardation and Developmental Disabilities and the Assembly Standing Committee on Codes," www.nyclu.org, April 8, 2005. Reproduced by permission.

New York Court of Appeals' decision in *Rivers v. Katz*, the Court stated that the modern trend in the legal and psychiatric fields is to give even those inpatients suffering from psychological disabilities an increasing amount of control over all of their treatment decisions—including what medication regimes he or she follows, what therapy sessions he or she attends, and what other mental health programs he or she participates in.

## Intrusive Invasions Serve No Purpose

Involuntary outpatient commitment (IOC) orders under Mental Hygiene Law typically involve judicial decrees that compel the administration of psychotropic drugs and require participation in other mental health services. These orders subject capable individuals to highly intrusive invasions of personal liberty and bodily integrity. According to the New York State Office of Mental Health, [these] orders absolutely determine what medications a capable person takes; where a capable person receives therapy, spends much of the day (day treatment or rehabilitative programs) and lives (such as a community residence with a curfew and many rules); and whether a capable person submits to blood and urine testing. As of April 1, 2005, there have been 4,044 such intrusive orders entered statewide and, according to [the] New York State Office of Mental Health,

- 88% of those orders direct a medication regimen,

- 75% of those orders direct participation in individual and/or group therapy,

- 40% of those orders direct participation in substance abuse programs,

- 37% of those orders direct participation in blood or urine testing,

- 31% of those orders direct participation in specific housing or housing support services, and

- 22% of those orders direct participation in specific day program services.

We respectfully submit that the New York State Office of Mental Health has submitted no evidence that the compulsion portion of "Kendra's Law" has served any purpose whatsoever. Indeed, the only benefit that the IOC order appears, at best, to confer on an individual, previously largely unserved, if served at all by the mental health system, is preferential access to scarce mental health resources. Thus, for example, 100% of IOC order recipients have received intensive case management services, 75% of IOC order recipients have received individual or group therapy, 22% of IOC order recipients have been able to access day programming services, 40% of IOC order recipients have been able to access substance abuse services, and 31% of IOC order recipients have been able to access housing and/or housing support services.

## Improve Quality of Care Instead of Forcing Services on People

All research on court-ordered mental health treatment demonstrates that the two most salient factors in reducing recidivism and problematic behavior among people with severe mental illness is access to enhanced services and access to enhanced case management/monitoring services. One of the most comprehensive and best-designed studies of outpatient commitment was carried out at New York City's Bellevue Hospital.

The Bellevue study found that court orders did not lead to increased patient compliance with treatment; did not lead to lower rates of hospitalizations; did not lead to lower rates of arrest or violent acts committed; and did not lead to reduction in symptoms or increase in functioning. Providing higher quality services and taking extra care to coordinate them was demonstrated to reduce the frequency of hospitalization. . . .

"Kendra's Law" ultimately poses a threat to the entire mental health system by removing patient trust. As patients become afraid of forced treatment they are less likely to seek treatment. And, ironically, treatment is also less likely to be available to those who voluntarily seek it. In a system in which treatment services are in short supply, the obligation to find services for those who are compelled to have them acts as a rationing device. There are already some areas in the State that are seeing critical shortages of intensive case managers because they are available only to people in outpatient commitment programs, and not to other people in the community who need them.

## Disturbing Disparities in Use of Law

The most disturbing information, however, provided by the New York State Office of Mental Health in its mandated final report to the Legislature on "Kendra's Law," reveals major racial/ethnic and geographic disparities throughout New York State in the implementation of "Kendra's Law." What have we learned about the operation of the statute over the past four years? We have learned that:

- Black people are almost five times as likely as White people to be the receipients of IOC orders.

- Hispanic people are two and a half times as likely as non-Hispanic White people to be the recipients of IOC orders.

- People who live in New York City are more than four times as likely to be the recipients of IOC orders as people living in the rest of the state.

- People with multiple psychiatric hospitalizations, but no histories of hurting others, are the primary recipients of IOC orders.

- New York City leads the state in using a state law that disproportionately takes away the freedom of certain people of color who are mentally ill.

The NYCLU is very troubled by what appears to be significant racial, ethnic and geographic disparities in the implementation of New York State's involuntary outpatient commitment law and by the failure of New York State and New York City to explain these disparities. The New York State Office of Mental Health has characterized, with no further comment or explanation, the racial and ethnic composition of the recipients of IOC orders as "diverse." According, to the New York State Office of Mental Health,

- 42% of IOC order recipients are Black,

- 34% of IOC order recipients are White, and

- 21% are Hispanic.

But, when compared with a similar population of mental health service recipients, the percentage of IOC order recipients who are men of color is disproportionate to the percentage of men of color whom the State has characterized as suffering from severe and persistent mental illness. Geographically, IOC orders are sought and imposed in a particularly skewed fashion across the state. As of April 1, 2005, New York City, Nassau and Suffolk Counties on Long Island and Erie County represented the locations where the majority of orders have been entered. Yet, the New York State Office of Mental Health has afforded no explanation as to why there is such stark geographic disparity in the application of "Kendra's Law."

- New York City (5 counties or boroughs) 3,078 orders,

- Nassau County 165 orders,

- Suffolk County 254 orders,

- 41 other counties combined 547, and

- 14 counties have entered no orders.

## Better Approaches Are Available

The statute, by its terms, expires on June 30, 2005. [In 2005 the law was extended for five years.] We submit that there are substantive issues concerning the implementation of "Kendra's Law." We urge the Legislature to ascertain precisely why there appears to have been such divergent racial, ethnic and geographic disparities in the implementation of "Kendra's Law." We hope, and expect, that in deliberating upon "Kendra's Law," the Legislature will strike a more appropriate balance between the interests of the state and the interests of the individual. And we urge the Legislature to examine a variety of alternative approaches to the compelled psychiatric treatment imposed on individuals under "Kendra's Law." For example, in 1999, Senator Libous proposed funding a statewide education and outreach program concerning the use of advanced directives and health care proxies by those persons with psychiatric disabilities. Assemblyman Brennan proposed enhancing coordination of existing and new services designed to engage a small group of individuals with psychiatric disabilities who have higher needs for supports and services than the general population of individuals suffering from psychiatric disabilities.

Kendra's Law violates the fundamental freedoms of competent, nondangerous persons with psychiatric disabilities who constitutionally could not be detained involuntarily in psychiatric facilities. Kendra's Law keeps these persons under the control of the State after they have been released. It prescribes for them involuntary and highly restrictive treatment programs and could force them to take medications against their will. Because the two most salient factors in reducing recidivism and problematic behavior among people with severe mental illness are enhanced services and enhanced monitoring, we strongly urge the Legislature to abandon the costly administrative mechanism that drives the geographic disparity and racial and socioeconomic biases evident in the implementation of "Kendra's Law" and devote those resources to affording New York State's citizens with severe mental illness access to the full range of appropriate enhanced psychiatric services.

# The Insanity Defense Is a Legitimate Legal Approach

## Mental Health America

*Mental Health America (formerly known as the National Mental Health Association) is a nonprofit organization that promotes mental wellness for the health and well-being of the nation.*

The National Mental Health Association (NMHA) is on record as supporting the maximum diversion from the criminal justice system of all persons accused of crimes for whom voluntary mental health treatment is a reasonable alternative to the use of criminal sanctions, at the earliest possible phase of the criminal process, preferably before booking or arraignment.

Further, NMHA has expressed skepticism concerning mental health court initiatives as they risk further criminalizing persons with mental illness. NMHA does not support mental health courts unless a particular court provides a meaningful alternative to criminal sanctions and meets the guidelines established in its position statement.

Historically, NMHA has been a leader in supporting the insanity defense. In July, 1982, when public interest was at its height following the acquittal of John Hinckley of the attempted assassination of President Reagan on grounds of not guilty by reason of insanity, NMHA convened a panel of experts to examine the insanity defense. The panel was known as the National Commission on the Insanity Defense. The Commission held public hearings, took testimony from more than twenty witnesses and, in March, 1983, submitted its report and recommendations, entitled "Myths and Realities: A Report of the National Commission on the Insanity Defense."

Mental Health America, "NMHA Policy Positions: In Support of the Insanity Defense," www.nmha.org, March 7, 2004. Reproduced by permission.

This policy is a restatement of those conclusions, supporting a broad form of the insanity defense.

## Insanity Defense Is Misunderstood

Society has long recognized the need for judges and juries to discern which defendants are "criminally responsible" for their acts and which are not. The insanity defense refers to a defendant's plea that he or she is not guilty of a crime because he or she lacked the mental capacity to appreciate that what she or he did was wrong.

There have been many well-publicized court cases (at the turn of the century) involving the insanity defense. These include the Andrea Yates case in Texas and the Russell Weston case in Washington, D.C. These cases involve individuals who had been diagnosed with a mental illness and who committed crimes resulting in tragedies. When such cases arise, there is usually a discussion about the use of the insanity defense, its usefulness to society, and whether or not an individual is "faking" a mental illness to avoid a prison sentence. The public perception of the insanity defense is that it is overused and exploited.

---

*An understanding was reached that the impaired emotional system of a person with serious mental illness going through a life crisis may not permit the person to appreciate the consequences of his or her act.*

---

The reality is that the insanity defense is rarely used. The defense is, inevitably, less successful when community feeling is high and, given the certainty of involuntary treatment, it is rarely used in minor crimes. The implication that the insanity defense is used by "fakers" is disputed by the fact that in 80 percent of the cases where a defendant is acquitted on a "not guilty by reason of insanity" plea, the prosecution and defense have agreed on the appropriateness of the plea before the trial.

Mental illness is real, serious and treatable. Failure to recognize this results in unnecessary criminalization of persons with mental illness. Recognition of a broad form of the insanity defense is essential for the judicial system to address these issues. . . .

## Origins of the Insanity Defense

The insanity defense goes back to M'Naughten's Case. [Daniel] M'Naughten attempted to kill the Prime Minister of England but mistakenly killed the Prime Minister's secretary. His motivation for this attempted assassination was his belief that the Prime Minister was involved in a conspiracy to kill him. Due to his incapacity to appreciate the difference between right and wrong, M'Naughten was acquitted.

---

*A person found not guilty should not be imprisoned, as a guilty person would be.*

---

Thus, from the origins of the insanity defense, considerations of morality were combined with the factual question of whether or not the accused rationally appreciated the consequences of his or her act. And though the language of M'Naughten's Case discouraged juries from focusing on noncognitive impairments, on the boundary between rational appreciation and moral appreciation, an understanding was reached that the impaired emotional system of a person with serious mental illness going through a life crisis may not permit the person to appreciate the consequences of his or her act. Mental illness now is understood to entail moral, rational and emotional impairments, all of which bear on guilt or innocence if they impair the persons's "substantial capacity" to "appreciate" the "wrongfulness" (the Model Penal Code's

Reporter's preferred term) or "criminality" of the person's act. Thus, the insights of psychiatry concerning personal responsibility found their way into the courtroom. But all of these formulations failed to address the final element: the ability for the individual to have volitional control over his or her conduct. This element was added in later case law and legislation. . . .

## Opposition to the Insanity Defense

The insanity defense has come under attack from several quarters, including the development of "guilty but insane" laws which deny the accused the right to claim insanity as a defense to the crime and permit only that the accused confess to the crime and seek to explain his or her conduct, requesting clemency through that process. This is the common traffic court plea of "guilty with an explanation." Yet people with mental illness who are convicted and treated pursuant to "guilty but insane" laws are not treated better, or granted any enforceable right to treatment. A tragic example of the misuse of the "guilty but insane" plea occurred in the Wilson case, in South Carolina. Such defendants are inappropriately saddled with a criminal conviction, even if they would have been not guilty by reason of insanity under the consensus test of the Model Penal Code. For those who argue that the mens rea defense survives, it should be understood that in crimes of negligence, there is no such defense. Thus, with guilty but insane, a conviction of some sort is assured, independent of the person's real responsibility/capacity. This seems profoundly unfair. Therefore, NMHA vigorously opposes "guilty but insane" laws. . . .

## Mental Illness Requires Compassionate Treatment

While beyond the scope of this policy, it is essential that successful invocation of the insanity defense be followed up with appropriate treatment as well as compassionate care during confinement and protection of human and civil rights. A person found not guilty should not be imprisoned, as a guilty person would be. It is also essential that recovery through treatment lead to release back to the community, although it is realistic to anticipate long delays in notorious cases. The treatment and release process should be removed from the criminal justice system and be placed in the clinical treatment process, and a comprehensive review of the person's mental health and recovery should be the basis for a finding of dangerousness or release.

# The Insanity Defense Is an Unacceptable Legal Approach

## Deroy Murdock

*Deroy Murdock is a New York-based columnist with the Scripps Howard news service and a senior fellow with the Atlas Economic Research Foundation in Arlington, Virginia.*

In the latest lunacy to blacken America's legal system, a lawyer representing John Hinckley asked a federal court to grant President Reagan's would-be assassin ten unsupervised visits to his parents' Williamsburg, Virginia home. Since the Secret Service monitors Hinckley, attorney Barry Levine told U.S. District Judge Paul Friedman November 17 [2003]: "Without doubt, he is the least dangerous person on the planet."

American juries need a new tool to stop such high-level madness. Federal and state lawmakers should empower jurors to find defendants "guilty but insane."

As it stands, the March 30, 1981 near-murder of Ronald Reagan, White House press secretary James Brady's brain trauma and resulting paralysis, Secret Service agent Timothy McCarthy's pierced liver, and Washington, D.C. policeman Thomas Delahanty's perforated neck all ... sort of ... just happened. Hinckley's claims of mental illness led a D.C. jury to find him not guilty by reason of insanity on June 21, 1982. This created the metaphysical anomaly wherein some 230 million Americans repeatedly watched news footage of these shootings while eyewitnesses saw police and Secret Service agents disarm Hinckley and whisk him to jail in manacles. And yet, magically, he was acquitted. So who pulled the trigger of Hinckley's Roehm .22-caliber revolver? Perhaps the ghost of Lee Harvey Oswald did it.

Deroy Murdock, "Legal Insanity: Let the Insane Be Gulity, Too," Nationalreview.com, November 20, 2003. Reproduced by permission of United Media Enterprises.

A guilty-but-insane verdict would offer several vital benefits.

The first is epistemological. Since Hinckley, now 48, was found not guilty of shooting four human beings, as a journalist, I hesitate to assert that he did so. Writing that Hinckley did something of which he was exonerated—although his culpability is otherwise universally accepted—potentially could expose me to libel charges. Such caution should be unnecessary. A guilty-but-insane verdict would let society, history, and the law declare specific perpetrators responsible for particular criminal acts. Victims of lawlessness and their families could comfort themselves in knowing that individuals were convicted for their wrongdoing.

---

*The "not guilty by reason of insanity" verdict is simply bananas.*

---

Second, a guilty-but-insane verdict would assure that the criminally insane experience long-term segregation from civilization. Rather than enjoy weekend getaways, unhinged gunmen ruled guilty but insane would receive as much psychiatric care as medicine and mercy merit. If they remained mentally ill, they would continue their treatment. If they regained their sanity, however, they promptly would be transferred to prison to endure the consequences of their misdeeds.

Third, since those who receive this verdict would follow clear paths from therapy to punishment, crime victims and their families would not have to suffer the emotional agony of watching these lawbreakers attend numerous hearings where their freedom is debated and sometimes granted. Such proceedings amplify the grief and anxiety of victims and survivors. This, in a word, is unjust.

It would be far better for the Bradys, Delahantys, McCarthys, and Reagans to sleep peacefully knowing that John Hinckley never will walk free again. Plagued by mental illness, he would get psychological attention. If and when he returns to mental health, however, he would get a one-way ride to a regular prison to serve a likely life sentence for almost killing the president of the United States, a key West Wing adviser, and two men dedicated to their protection.

So how is Hinckley handling all this? Not swimmingly, according to President Reagan's son.

Hinckley's doctors—Ron Reagan Jr. said on ABC News November 17—"took a look in his cell and found out he was pen pals with [serial killer] Ted Bundy, [Unabomber] Ted Kaczynski, Charlie Manson, I believe, and they found a stash of photographs of Jodie Foster," the Academy-Award-winning actress who Hinckley aimed to impress by shooting Reagan.

"Psychiatry is a guessing game, and I do my best to keep the fools guessing about me," Hinckley wrote in his diary in 1987. "They will never know the true John Hinckley. Only I fully understand myself."

John Hinckley is either crazy or crazy like a fox. But the "not guilty by reason of insanity" verdict is simply bananas, as this latest hearing proves beyond a reasonable doubt. Justice requires a guilty-but-insane finding so that tomorrow's John Hinckleys stay either in straitjackets or prison stripes, not at their parents' homes or—worse—on the prowl for fresh prey.

# The Juvenile Mental Health System Does Not Work

*Sam Rosenfeld*

*Sam Rosenfeld writes for the* American Prospect.

For thousands of children with debilitating mental illnesses, the get-tough juvenile-justice culture of the 1990s could not have come at a worse time. The new punitive policies emerged in tandem with the slow breakdown of the public mental-health system, and the confluence has led to a pervasive criminalization of juvenile mental illness.

The excesses of the "super-predator"–era juvenile-justice policies are well-known, but just as damaging were the shift in focus and resources they signaled. Punishment came to replace rehabilitation as the core goal of the American juvenile-justice system at the same time that our mental-health system was sinking into a sustained crisis. The failure of community-based mental-health care to meet the needs of children in the wake of national deinstitutionalization served to push mentally ill kids into the juvenile-justice system—in effect, to *reinstitutionalize* them, this time into a system woefully ill-equipped to help.

In the last 15 years, matters have grown worse, primarily because of the way states have responded to the shortage of mental-health services. Instead of addressing the problem directly, too many states embarked on a roller-coaster engagement with private, managed-care Medicaid providers who promised that cost cutting and streamlining could mitigate the need for more mental-health resources and services. State after state eventually discovered the perils of such arrangements. Sweetheart contracts gave for-profit HMOs few incentives for service quality. Savings were eaten up by enormous administrative costs and fat profit margins. Care was slashed and services denied, more acutely in mental health than anywhere else.

## In Jail Instead of Counseling

Meanwhile, the number of youths entering the juvenile-justice system increased substantially over the 1990s. The new get-tough laws played a large role in that, but some of the rise was related to the problems in mental-health treatment. The Texas Youth Commission, for instance, found a 27-percent increase in the number of kids with mental disorders entering the state juvenile-justice system from 1995 to 2001. "It's a hydraulic effect," says George Davis, director of the University of New Mexico's Division of Child & Adolescent Psychiatry, who helped pioneer mental-health reforms in Albuquerque's juvenile-detention system. "This population exists no matter what, and if they're not in treatment facilities, they're in detention. When one goes down, the other goes up."

Estimates vary regarding the proportion of detained youth suffering from mental disorders. Northwestern University Medical School's Linda Teplin and colleagues have studied mental-illness prevalence among detained youth in Chicago. In 2002, they reported that nearly 60 percent of male detainees and 67 percent of females suffered from at least one psychiatric disorder.

Moreover, there is increasingly robust evidence that the juvenile-justice system serves as a dumping ground for mentally ill children lacking health services. The National Alliance for the Mentally Ill (NAMI) commissioned a poll of families of children with mental illness in 1999 and found that more than a third of respondents reported placing their kids in the juvenile-justice system in order to access mental-health services. A series of investigations in 2002 and 2004 carried out by Congressman Henry Waxman's minority staff of the House Government Reform Committee addressed this issue. Their report, published last summer, analyzed responses from more than 500 juvenile-detention administrators representing 75 percent of all detention facilities in the country. It found that two-thirds of the facilities held children who were awaiting community mental-health treatment. In 33 states, facilities held mentally ill youth who had no charges against them.

At a Senate hearing highlighting the report, one witness, Carol Carothers, executive director of NAMI's Maine chapter, recounted stories of mentally ill youth in her state shunted into the juvenile-justice system. One 18-year-old whose mental illness had gone untreated for years eventually hanged himself in the state's "supermax" prison. Another youth, 13, had enjoyed treatment and counseling in a residential program until his mother, a member of a NAMI support group, moved north. "The plans to link him to new services fell apart," Carothers testified, "and he ended up with nothing—no psychiatrist, no caseworker, no medications, and no therapist. As one would expect, he fell apart and landed in juvenile detention, where he still is." According to the mother, the child first began to cut himself and act violently while in detention.

Addressing the crisis of mental illness in juvenile justice means grappling with the dysfunctions of two extremely complex and diverse systems. But several localities have shown how reform can happen.

## One Man Makes a Difference in New Mexico

As much as any other state, New Mexico epitomized the trends of the 1990s that had left mentally ill children stranded in the juvenile-justice system. A Republican administration initiated a litany of get-tough youth policies, including mandatory sentencing, state-run boot camps, and the construction of a $ 7.5 million maximum-security juvenile prison in Albuquerque. Meanwhile, the state's experience with managed care for mental health, implemented in 1997, was typically disastrous. The system's byzantine structure sucked 45 percent of all funding into administrative costs while services were slashed and reimbursement rates plummeted. Not surprisingly, the warehousing of juveniles with untreated mental-health needs in detention centers became an acute problem. An investigation by Waxman's team found that in 2001, one in seven youths in New Mexico's detention centers were there primarily due to the lack of available mental-health services.

In the midst of all this, one pioneering reformer spearheaded an overhaul of the largest detention system in the state, in Bernalillo County (encompassing Albuquerque). Tom Swisstack, formerly the mayor of a fast-growing Albuquerque suburb, took the reins of the detention center in 1998. With his intense drive, he commenced his reform campaign in 2000 with support from the Annie E. Casey Foundation's innovative juvenile-detention reform initiative. Replicating many features of the original Casey Foundation sites, the Bernalillo reforms focused on new, sophisticated screening procedures to place nondangerous offenders in home- and community-based alternatives to detention. During a June visit to the center's premises in dusty northwestern Albuquerque, I went step by step through the processes of booking, assessment, and individualized service, with Swisstack highlighting the myriad methods by which children get diverted into the two home-based supervision programs run by the center.

Adding to the basic Casey Foundation model, Swisstack applies an innovative focus on serving the mental-health needs of the children in the system. On top of intensive staff training and new therapeutic programs to provide a continuum of care, he has also negotiated agreements with the state's three Medicaid managed-care providers to reimburse counseling and medication services for kids with mental-health needs. This led to the construction in 2001 of a community mental-health clinic on the detention center's premises—the only such clinic in the country. In addition to the clinic's case managers, psychologists, and psychiatrists, three full-time clinicians now treat the residential population in the detention center itself, and Swisstack is looking to hire more.

---

*A serious national commitment to providing community-based mental-health services and coordinated systems of care is needed.*

---

"I now have a clinical staff that is actually implementing programs in a proactive rather than reactive approach," says a gratified Swisstack. Importantly, these benefits extend far beyond the detained youth: Albuquerque's clinic serves the mental-health needs of others in the community, too. During my visit, I met Tonya and her 10-year-old son, Charles (their names have been changed). Charles, whose father died when he was 3, suffered violent, uncontrollable outbursts at home and school. Two years ago, his school referred him to the mental-health clinic, where he was quickly diagnosed as bipolar. He now receives medication and meets weekly with a psychiatrist at the clinic for counseling; Medicaid covers both. Tonya called the treatment "a Iifesaver," and reflected on what might have happened if the clinic's services weren't available. "The juvenile jail's right next door," she said, "and every week I drive in here and think, 'If it wasn't for this place, he might be over there.'"

## States Skeptical of Managed Care

Certain political conditions have helped Swisstack's efforts, and those of other reformers in the country. State and local fiscal strains have made officials much more amenable to cheaper alternatives to incarceration. Meanwhile, the first, disastrous cycle of state experiments with managed care has run its course and provoked closer public scrutiny, and many states are beginning to be much stricter about the requirements included in new contracts. Swisstack is now in negotiations with a newly contracted statewide managed-care provider to cover seven more mental-health-clinic sites across the state. As the University of New Mexico's George Davis explains, the prospects for such an agreement are better now because the company actually has strong contractual incentives to provide treatment. "The state has really wised up . . . [and] is going to watch them closely," he says. "This time the contract at least makes some sense."

For all the good such reforms do, however, this crisis is fundamentally an outgrowth of the broken public mental-health system itself. Neither detention reforms, nor other promising juvenile-justice innovations, nor smarter managed-care contracts are going to be enough to fix that. A serious national commitment to providing community-based mental-health services and coordinated systems of care is needed—and realizing that goal remains well beyond the capacity of juvenile-justice reformers alone.

# The Managed Care Approach to Health Care Blocks Access to Mental Health Treatment

*Samuel E. Menaged*

*Samuel E. Menaged is president and CEO of the Renfrew Center in Philadelphia, a residential facility dedicated to the treatment of women with eating disorders.*

Unless you have faced it in your own family, it is difficult to describe the upheaval and pain that accompanies mental illness. So, let us paint a picture.

Imagine your daughter or wife suffers from anorexia and bulimia. She weighs just 92 pounds, about 80% of her ideal body weight. She eats less than 300 calories a day, the equivalent of two pieces of bread and a slice of cheese. If she eats any more than her self-imposed calorie limit, she then "purges" by forcing herself to vomit. She is weak, emaciated, and beginning to show the signs of malnourishment, including cardiac problems. Emotionally, she is crippled. She cannot work or attend school. She is ravaged by anxiety and depression. She is unable to participate in a relationship.

Make no mistake, her eating disorder is not a lifestyle choice. She is the victim of a disease, just as a cancer patient is. There is a difference, however, one that can ultimately be deadly for the victim of mental disease—treatment for her sickness is often not covered by health insurance.

## Mental Health Costs Are Difficult to Predict

As managed care has increased its hold on the American health care system, mental health has become one of its most-beaten victims. To reduce spiraling costs, insurers often look at men-

Samuel E. Menaged, "Obstacles to Accessing Mental Health Care," *USA Today*, March 2003, p. 30. Copyright © 2003 Society for the Advancement of Education. Reproduced by permission.

tal health benefits as the first place to cut. In fact, from an actuarial perspective, mental health costs are among the most difficult to predict and therefore the most risky. Each course of treatment can be wildly different from patient to patient. For example, a person suffering from depression may respond well to drug therapy with minimal need for professional "talk" therapy—the more-expensive component in the treatment mix. However, another patient with the same level of severity may require several medications and ongoing psychotherapy over the course of many months or even years.

While some health plans have eliminated or drastically reduced benefits, other insurers outsource the administration of mental health benefits to companies that specialize in the management of such benefits. In these scenarios, the company acting as administrator operates under a "risk contract," meaning it contracts with providers and hospitals to administer 100% of the mental health care necessary for a certain number of insurance subscribers. In return, the administrator receives a fixed dollar amount. Any monies left over after the provision of care go into the pockets of the administrator. Therefore, the less care the administrator has to pay therapists and hospitals to provide, the more money it makes. So, it is easy to see how the administrator may define "necessity" for care differently than a health care provider, patient, or patient's family.

As it stands, private companies use their own definitions of "necessity" to determine whether or not a patient should receive treatment. Often, the attending psychiatrist or therapist may deem that treatment is necessary, or guidelines set forth by the American Psychiatric Association may indicate the need for a particular level of care. Nevertheless, the insurer will deny the benefit.

"The greatest fight in the treatment of mental illness isn't only improving the physical and emotional health of patients; it is also the constant effort to move patients' own insurance companies toward a better understanding of their illnesses, so they will remove the barriers to effective care," says Gayle Brooks, vice president of The Renfrew Center, the nation's largest network of mental health facilities dedicated to eating disorder treatment.

---

*The day before her authorization expired, the girl's therapist learned that significant family issues compounded her eating disorder—she had been the victim of sexual abuse from a close relative.*

---

## Preventive Medicine for Mental Health

Even when mental health benefits exist, accessing them can prove nearly impossible because the criteria imposed by insurance companies or benefit administrators may be dangerously restrictive. When it comes to inpatient care or psychiatric hospitalization, the battle can be even more difficult because many insurance companies just cover inpatient care when it is deemed a "medical necessity"—that is, when persons pose an immediate threat to themselves or others. For a person suffering from depression, medical necessity may be a suicide attempt. For a person suffering from anorexia, medical necessity may be a heart attack, loss of consciousness, or falling below 75% of ideal body weight.

Two distinct problems arise by using medical necessity as the primary criterion for admission to a mental health facility. First, medical necessity often presents itself after an episode that can prove fatal or debilitating on its own. If a depressed person succeeds in committing suicide or an eating disorder patient dies from malnutrition, the medical necessity criteria is moot. By contrast, diseases that solely affect the body are treated with prophylactic approaches to avoid dangerous episodes: People with high blood pressure are prescribed medication; individuals with coronary blockages undergo bypass surgery; and those with cancer risks are tested for the presence of the disease. Patients suffering the symptoms of mental disease do not receive the same level of care.

The second problem is that, even when the condition of medical necessity is satisfied, the mental disease is often not cured. For this reason, recurrence of symptoms is frequently seen as well as repeat acute episodes, and these acute episodes require second, third, or fourth hospitalizations.

## Barriers to Care

In the case of eating disorders, victims are often in and out of hospital emergency rooms. Had they been treated at the time of the first episode, their chances of recurrence would have been drastically reduced. However, insurance companies frequently deny benefits prior to the completion of treatment. In some cases, they not only deny coverage, but refuse to let their subscribers pay for their own treatment.

At an incident at The Renfrew Center, an adolescent girl suffering from anorexia was approved by her insurance company for admission into the Center's Philadelphia facility for a three-day stay. Its therapists advocated for the patient to continue in her treatment, and the insurance company approved an additional seven days of inpatient care. The day before her authorization expired, the girl's therapist learned that significant family issues compounded her eating disorder—she had been the victim of sexual abuse from a close relative. In light of the revelation, Renfrew's professional staff requested that the insurance company authorize payment for an extension of treatment. The request was denied.

---

*Insurance companies create their own criteria of "necessity" rooted more in fundamentals of economics than in fundamentals of mental health.*

---

Unwilling to discharge the patient at this critical stage of her recovery, Renfrew substantially reduced its daily hospitalization charge to a nominal amount so that the girl's family could pay out of its own pocket for her treatment. After the patient's discharge, the insurance company learned of the payment arrangement and, because their contract stipulates that a provider cannot accept money from a patient after coverage has been denied, they demanded that the Center refund the family's payments. Working to preserve its relationship with the insurance company, Renfrew complied with this demand, effectively providing two weeks of treatment at its own expense. Shortly thereafter, the insurer terminated its contract with the organization anyway.

Treatment facilities and hospitals face these battles every day. If they choose to help a person whose coverage is denied, they risk losing insurance contracts that are vital to keeping these facilities in operation. If they choose not to help these victims, they are turning their backs on people with severe mental diseases in search of help and guidance.

## What Can Be Done?

Currently, victims of mental illness, their families, and the professionals who provide treatment face four main obstacles. These need to be eliminated in order for patients to access the care they require.

**Determination of treatment.** Prior to the introduction of managed care contracting, it was up to the team of professionals directly involved in the patient's care to make decisions about the course of treatment, not distant insurance company employees who, more often than not, have little experience with mental health issues and often have no experience with specific mental diseases. The American Psychiatric Association has set guidelines to determine the appropriate level of care required given certain criteria. Yet, insurance companies often ignore these standards (the same ones employed by professional therapists). Instead, insurance companies create their own criteria of "necessity" rooted more in fundamentals of economics than in fundamentals of mental health.

**The right to pay privately.** As indicated in the earlier anecdote, some managed care companies refuse to let their subscribers pay for their own treatment, even after the insurer has denied continued treatment. Others forbid private payment until the patient has exhausted all appeals. That can take days or even weeks, leaving patients in limbo about their treatment and undermining the continuity of care that is so critical to them. This clause is written into managed care contracts, and treatment providers cannot accept the patient's payment.

**Exclusion of specific diseases.** Some insurance polices exclude specific diseases, eating disorders being the most commonly cited. Most people would cry "discrimination" if AIDS were excluded by a health plan. Similarly, it is discrimination to exclude any disease recognized as a mental illness by the Diagnostic and Statistical Manual of Mental Disorders, Fourth Edition.

**Lack of parity between medical/surgical care and mental health care.** Society has accepted the pervasive belief—albeit incorrect—that mental health care is not essential; that mental illness, even if untreated, cannot lead to death. Unfortunately for thousands of victims of eating disorders, acute depression, and other mental diseases, this is far from true. Mental illnesses can and do kill. Nonetheless, insurance companies have not treated mental health and medical/surgical care equitably. For instance, many insurance plans offer in excess of $1,000,000 of medical/surgical benefits, but limit mental health benefits to 30 outpatient sessions or 10 days of inpatient care.

There is, perhaps, a glimmer of light at the end of the tunnel. The Mental Health Equitable Treatment Act of 2001, proposed by Senators Paul Wellstone (D.-Minn.) and Pete Domenici (R.-N.M.), aims to create parity between mental and medical health. Unlike its predecessor, the Mental Health Parity Act of 1996, it would not allow insurance plans to impose arbitrary caps on inpatient days and outpatient visits. Also, health plans would no longer be able to charge higher copayment and deductible amounts for treatment for mental illness. Passed by the Senate in October, 2001, the act would provide full parity for all categories of mental health conditions listed in the Diagnostic and Statistical Manual of Mental Disorders, Fourth Edition with coverage contingent on the mental health condition being included in an authorized treatment plan.

The Mental Health Equitable Treatment Act of 2001 was set to take the Congressional floor in September, 2001, but was postponed as the result of the terrorist attacks on the World Trade Center and Pentagon. It appears that, in the wake of the attacks and the weakened economy, despite the fact that mental health needs have grown substantially since Sept. 11, fewer legislators are comfortable with a law that may have a negative short-term impact on insurance companies. As a result, the act is stuck in committee in the House and it is possible that it may never emerge. [As of January 2007, this act has still not been voted into law.]

While the new legislation would offer hope to millions of Americans that they will have greater access to mental health care, professionals in the trenches working with victims of mental illness insist there are other steps that must be met, especially if the act dies in the House: Adopt the guidelines of the American Psychiatric Association as they relate to medical necessity for treating mental illness; guarantee the patient's right to pay privately; and end the discrimination that excludes certain diseases from mental health insurance policies.

When someone is sick, whether from a disease that can be seen under a microscope or from one that strikes the mind invisibly, treatment is required. Unfortunately for such individuals, the current system for providing treatment for those invisible diseases of the mind remains painfully and dangerously troubled. If we are to ask patients with mental illness to face their demons, then, as a society, we must eliminate the demons that stand in their way.

# Screening Helps Prevent Teen Suicide

## Ellie Ashford

*Ellie Ashford is editor of the National School Boards Association's School Board News.*

A school health official tells of a high-achieving ninth-grade girl who, for no apparent reason, began doing poorly in school and made a suicide attempt. Her parents had no idea what was wrong.

After she took part in a voluntary mental health screening program, it was revealed that she had been raped a year earlier and had told no one about it. The screening allowed the student to get immediate assistance from a mental health professional.

It is stories like this that proponents of mental health screening point to in illustrating the benefits of screening seemingly healthy teenagers.

Yet, there is growing opposition to mental health screening, with one school health expert calling the practice "as controversial as sex education."

## Strong Views on Screening

Among the anti-screening groups are the Church of Scientology, which is opposed to psychiatry and psychotropic drugs, and Christian conservative groups, who oppose governmental usurpation of parental authority and view screening as a plot by pharmaceutical companies to expand their markets to schoolchildren.

Concerned Women for America, for example, says "medicating children for behavioral problems could easily become a form of social control. . . . School authorities could use medication to prevent behavior of which they simply disapproved, such as rebelliousness."

The group refers to screening as the first step toward the practice used by Soviet and Chinese communists to label political dissidents as mentally ill.

Pressure by anti-screening forces has led to legislation restricting mental health screening in schools to be proposed in 10 states, the National Mental Health Association reports.

Those who support screening liken it to health services already carried out in schools, such as vaccinations and vision and hearing tests. And they say screening is an important tool in promoting mental health and preventing suicide.

A federally funded study recently reported that more than 46 percent of all Americans will have at least one mental disorder at some point in their life, such as depression, anxiety disorders, impulse-control disorders, or drug or alcohol dependency.

Half of all mental illnesses begin by age 14, and three-fourths by age 24. Yet these disorders often go undiagnosed, which means many children aren't getting the treatment they need to live healthy lives.

Much of the controversy over mental health screening stems from an endorsement of the practice by the President's New Freedom Commission on Mental Health.

The commission's report, issued in 2003, includes among its many recommendations one to: "Improve and expand school mental health programs."

According to the report, "Quality screening and early intervention will occur in both readily accessible, low-stigma settings, such as primary health care facilities and schools, and in settings in which a high level of risk exists for mental health problems, such as criminal justice, juvenile justice, and child welfare systems."

## Federal Legislation on Screening

Last fall, President Bush signed into law a suicide prevention bill proposed by Sen. Gordon H. Smith (R-Ore.) that authorizes mental health screening.

The Garrett Lee Smith Memorial Act, named for Smith's son, who took his own life in 2003, includes a 10-state pilot program that allows states to develop youth suicide prevention and intervention programs, including screening. This program was funded at $10 million this year.

---

*We're not aware of any group in favor of mandatory, universal screening.*

---

Rep. Ron Paul (R-Texas), a vocal critic of mental health screening, has proposed an amendment to the House appropriations bill to ban the use of federal funding for screening. . . .

Jeff Deist, a spokesperson for Paul, calls mental health screening "another way for the government to interfere with the role of parent and child. It's a privacy issue."

He also raises concerns about having private information on a child's school record and increasing the number of children given psychotropic drugs.

"It is important to understand that powerful interests, namely federal bureaucrats and pharmaceutical lobbies, are behind the push for mental health screening in schools," Paul writes in his weekly column to constituents. "The pharmaceutical industry is eager to sell psychotropic drugs to millions of new customers in American schools."

## Teen Screen Is Not Sinister

Even though the proponents of mental health screening say it should always be voluntary and should never be done without parental consent, the opponents of screening continue to talk about "mandatory, universal screening."

"We're not aware of any group in favor of mandatory, universal screening," says Robert Caruano, co-director of Teen Screen. "Right-wing anti-government groups and anti-public school groups deliberately spread rumors that there is a plot to carry out mandatory screening without parental consent purely to make a political point, to send a political message to scare people."

Teen Screen is "not part of a nefarious, sinister plan," Caruano says. "We're not connected with the drug companies or the Bush Administration."

Teen Screen, created by Columbia University in New York City, is the most widely used mental health screening program. It is being used in more than 350 sites across the United States, two-thirds of them schools, Caruano says.

## A Simple Aim: Preventing Suicide

Teen Screen, designed for youths ages 11–18, is solely aimed at preventing teen suicide. He points to research by the Centers for Disease Control and Prevention that shows 17 percent of youths in grades 9–12 have had thoughts about killing themselves, 9 percent have attempted suicide, and 3 percent have taken actions so serious, they required medical attention.

He says 1,700 youths ages 15–19 commit suicide every year. Among youths ages 10–24, the number rises to 3,000. Suicide is the third highest cause of death among teens.

Teen Screen is free for agencies that qualify. Agencies interested in having a Teen Screen program must submit a signed letter from mental health providers ensuring that any student who needs assistance will be seen by a professional immediately.

The program is voluntary, and participants must have parental consent. The screening can be done either on a computer or with a paper-and-pencil instrument.

When a screening shows a student might be depressed, the professional giving the screening decides whether a full evaluation is needed, notifies a parent, and makes an appointment with a therapist.

## Teen Screen Works

Teen Screen is a "very effective" program, and "we've never had any complaints or controversies," says Marian Sheridan, coordinator of health and safety for the Fond du Lac, Wis., school district and coordinator of the Fond du Lac County School Health Initiative.

---

*Teens often have a way of internalizing their disorders. Usually you can't look at someone and tell if they're depressed.*

---

The district began using Teen Screen in 2002 for ninth-graders at Fond du Lac High School, and now uses it at a second district high school, two alternative schools, and a private school.

The program is incorporated into the ninth-grade health curriculum and is carried out as a "community-school commitment," Sheridan says. Students and their parents must sign a consent form before they can be screened.

At Fond du Lac High School, 358 of the school's 632 freshmen participated in the screening the last time it was given, she says. Sixty-four students had "screened positive," which means they are given clinical interviews the same day, and 55 of that group were referred for additional services. About half were referred to mental health services in the community, the rest to the school psychologist or guidance counselor.

School nurses who serve as case managers work with parents to identify mental health professionals covered by parents' insurance. They also make three follow-up contacts with students and parents to ensure that they've gotten the help they needed.

"Research shows we're most effective in finding and identifying kids you wouldn't know have a problem," Caruano says. Teens often have a way of "internalizing their disorders," he says. "Usually you can't look at someone and tell if they're depressed."

After a teenager commits suicide, Caruano says, people often say things like: "We had no idea he had any problems. He was on the honor roll. He seemed happy." According to Caruano, when a therapist asks a teen, "Why didn't you tell anyone how you felt?" the answer often is "nobody ever asked us." He says Teen Screen opens a door for troubled youths: "A lot of kids are looking for a way to open the door to their parents. They don't know how to bring it up."

The only other major screening initiative is the SOS High School Suicide Prevention Program, developed by a nonprofit organization called Screening for Mental Health Inc., which includes an instrument that teaches students how to recognize the signs of suicide in themselves and others and take appropriate action.

Approximately 1,700 public schools have participated in the program, says a spokesperson for the organization. It differs from Teen Screen in that students take and review the screens themselves. . . .

## Screening Is Not Perfect

Even some school mental health experts see some weaknesses in the screening concept.

"The notion of public schools doing screening as benign is naïve," says one school health specialist, who cites concerns about privacy and the possibility of overmedication. And although the ideal screening program should have sufficient staffing and resources so a troubled student can get immediate assistance, that might not always be the case.

"You are sending them somewhere else. You have no way of knowing whether they show up," says Louise Johnson, director of children's services for the South Carolina Department of Mental Health.

South Carolina leads the nation in the number of mental health professionals in public schools, Johnson says. More than half of the state's 1,000 schools have a trained clinician, mostly with a social work background.

These professionals, known as "counselors" so students aren't stigmatized for seeing them, meet with students individually, in groups, or with their families. They can address a wide range of problems, and can provide immediate referrals to any youths who appear suicidal, Johnson says.

Yet not all states and communities are able to make such a major commitment to mental health. Youth suicide is a serious problem, and many school health specialists believe the benefits of screening outweigh the risks.

# Mental Illness Screening for Teenagers Benefits Drug Companies Alone

*Evelyn Pringle*

*Evelyn Pringle is a columnist for Independent Media TV and an investigative journalist focused on government corruption.*

The scheme concocted by the pharmaceutical industry and pushed forward by the Bush administration to screen the entire nation's public school population for mental illness and treat them with controversial drugs . . . [has been] setting off alarms among parents all across the country. . . .

Tax-payers had better get out their check books because school taxes are about to go up as the lawsuits against school boards start mounting over the TeenScreen depression survey being administered to children in the school.

The first notice of intent to sue was filed . . . [in 2005] in Indiana by Michael and Teresa Rhoades, who were outraged when they learned their daughter had been given a psychological test at school without their consent.

In December 2004, their daughter came home from school and said she had been diagnosed with an obsessive compulsive and social anxiety disorder after taking the TeenScreen survey.

Teresa Rhoades always viewed her daughter as a happy normal teenager. "I was absolutely outraged that my daughter was told she had these two conditions based off a computer test," said Rhoades. . . .

Evelyn Pringle, "Teen Screen: The Lawsuit Begins," *Counterpunch*, June 13, 2005. Reproduced by permission.

## TeenScreen Diagnoses a Host of Disorders

Teresa and Michael Rhoades claim the survey was erroneous, improper, and done with reckless disregard for their daughter's welfare and that they did not give the school permission to give the test.

The parents allege that when their daughter took the test, she was improperly diagnosed with obsessive compulsive disorder and social anxiety disorder. That diagnosis, they claim, caused both the teen and her parents emotional distress, and the family intends to seek the "maximum amount of damages."

The Indiana child was diagnosed with two disorders in one crack but there are many more.

If a teen doesn't like doing math assignments, parents should not worry. TeenScreen may determine that the child simply has a mental illness known as developmental-arithmetic disorder.

There's also a diagnosis for those children who like to argue with their parents, they may be afflicted with a mental illness known [as] oppositional-defiant disorder.

And for anybody critical of the above 2 disorders, they may be suffering [from] the mental illness called noncompliance-with-treatment disorder.

No kidding, these illnesses are included in the more than 350 "mental disorders" listed in the American Psychiatric Association's Diagnostic and Statistical Manual of Mental Disorders, the insurance billing bible for mental disorders.

## TeenScreen Gets Tax Dollars

In addition to lawsuits, tax dollars are already funding Teen-Screen and many of the drugs purchased by the new customers it recruits.

While promoting TeenScreen to Congress, its Executive Director, Laurie Flynn, flat out lied when she told members of congress that TeenScreen was free and its website statement that "The program does not receive financial support from the government and is not affiliated with, or funded by, any pharmaceutical companies," is also a blatant lie.

On Oct 21, 2004 Bush authorized $82 million for suicide prevention programs like TeenScreen and a report in *Psychiatric Times* said the administration had proposed an increase in the budget for the Center for Mental Health Service from $862 million in 2004 to $912 million in fiscal 2005. TeenScreen is sure to get a cut of those tax dollars.

Federal tax dollars are also being funneled through state governments to fund TeenScreen. On Nov 17, 2004, Officials at the University of South Florida Department of Child & Family Studies said $98,641 was awarded to expand the TeenScreen program in the Tampa Bay area.

In Ohio, under the governor's Executive Budget for 2006 and 2007, the Department of Mental Health . . . specifically earmarked $70,000 for TeenScreen for each of those years, reports investigator Sue Weibert.

---

*Here's how this part of the scheme works. The drug companies bribe state officials and donate money in the form of "educational grants" to the states to approve . . . drug programs.*

---

[In] June 2002 the Update Newsletter published by the Tennessee Department of Mental Health, reported that 170 Nashville students had completed a TeenScreen survey. The Newsletter said the survey was funded by grants from AdvoCare and Eli Lilly. Last I knew, Eli Lilly was a pharmaceutical company.

The great news for Pharma was that 96 of the 170 students who took the survey ended up speaking to a therapist which no doubt resulted in the recruitment of 96 new pill-popping teens.

# Drug Companies Get Millions of Tax Dollars

Unbeknownst to many, taxpayers are already paying an enormous price as a result of marketing schemes designed to get students hooked on antipsychotic drugs. A list of drugs that must be prescribed for kids is already set up, modeled after a list used in Texas since 1995 called the TMAP. The list contains the most expensive drugs on the market.

In 2002, national sales of antipsychotics reached $6.4 billion in 2002, making them the fourth-highest-selling class of drugs, according to IMS Health, a company that tracks drug sales, in the May 2003, *New York Times*. By 2004, sales had jumped by over $2 billion with antipsychotics sales totaling $8.8 billion—$2.4 billion of which was paid for by state Medicaid funds, according to the May/June 2005 issue of *Mother Jones Magazine*.

Here's how this part of the scheme works. The drug companies bribe state officials and donate money in the form of "educational grants" to the states to approve and implement these TMAP drug programs, and then in return, state Medicaid programs fund the cost of the drugs with tax dollars.

For instance, in Texas, Pfizer awarded $232,000 in grants to the Texas department of mental health to "educate" mental health providers about TMAP, and in return, the Texas Medicaid program spent $233 million tax dollars on Pfizer drugs like Zoloft.

Johnson & Johnson (Janssen Pharmaceutica) gave grants of $224,000 to Texas and Medicaid spent $272 million on J & J antipsychotic drug, Risperdal.

Eli Lilly awarded $109,000 in grants to "educate" state mental health providers and as a result, Texas Medicaid spent $328 million for Lilly's antipsychotic drug Zyprexa.

The TMAP was approved in Texas in 1995, and by February 9, 2001, an article in the *Dallas Morning News*, titled "State Spending More on Mental Illness Drugs" reported: "Texas now spends more money on medication to treat mental illness for low-income residents than on any other type of prescription drug."

In addition to covering nearly 40% of the drugs for Medicaid recipients, the state also spends about another $60 million a year on "hundreds of thousands of prescription drugs for other state-funded programs at the Texas Department of Mental Health and Mental Retardation and the Texas Department of Criminal Justice," the paper reported.

---

*People are particularly worried about saving the children from senseless and dangerous drugging.*

---

By the time the 2002–2003 budget was established, Texas lawmakers had to increase the amount of money allocated to the department of health and human services by $1 billion with a significant portion earmarked for prescription drugs, according to Texas officials.

In 1999, Ohio adopted its version of TMAP and by 2002 Ohio's Medicaid program was spending $145 million on schizophrenia medications alone.

California spent over $500 million on the Atypicals Risperdal, Zyprexa and Seroqual in 2003.

In 2002, Missouri Medicaid spent $104 million on three TMAP drugs alone. The three topped the list of all other medications covered by Medicaid, including HIV, cancer, and heart drugs. . . .

## Trying to Save the Children

Dire warnings against mass mental health screening are coming from every segment of society, including parents, physicians, academics, journalists, and human rights groups because the influence of the pharmaceutical industry in this scheme is so patently obvious.

People are particularly worried about saving the children from senseless and dangerous drugging. According to long-time anti-child drugging advocate Doyle Mills, "Psychiatry has a long history of abject failure. Psychiatric treatments—drugs, electroconvulsive therapy, lobotomies—have harmed millions and robbed them of any hope of a normal life."

Expert records researcher Ken Kramer, who has been fighting against child drugging for years, has conducted a research project on child suicides in Florida that determined that medicating kids with the types of dangerous mind-altering drugs on these lists is causing suicide. He helped defeat TeenScreen's attempt to gain access to schools in 2 of Florida's largest counties. Ken has a TeenScreen website at http://www.psychsearch.net/teenscreen.html.

Dr Karen Effrem, a pediatrician and strong opponent of mandatory screening, recently warned, "Universal mental health screening and the drugging of children . . . needs to be stopped so that many thousands if not millions of children will be saved from receiving stigmatizing diagnoses that would follow them for the rest of their lives. America's school children should not be medicated by expensive, ineffective, and dangerous medications based on vague and dubious diagnoses."

In a letter to the editor in the *Washington Times* on October 31, 2004, Effrem summed up the dangers of using tax dollars to fund mass mental health screening of children: "Given the very real problems of already existing coercion, subjective criteria, dangerous and ineffective medication, and the failure of screening to prevent suicide . . . Congress would be wise to withhold the $44 million requested for state grants."

The nation's first lawsuit has been filed, and let it serve as a warning to other schools across the country to think twice before allowing the TeenScreen recruitment scheme to zero in on their students.

# Organizations to Contact

*The editors have compiled the following list of organizations concerned with the issues debated in this book. The descriptions are derived from materials provided by the organizations. All have publications or information available for interested readers. The list was compiled on the date of publication of the present volume; the information provided here may change. Be aware that many organizations take several weeks or longer to respond to inquiries, so allow as much time as possible.*

**American Association of Suicidology (AAS)**
5221 Wisconsin Avenue NW, Washington, DC   20015
(202) 237-2280 • fax: (202) 237-2282
e-mail: info@suicidology.org
Web site: www.suicidology.org

The association is one of the largest suicide prevention organizations in the nation. It believes that suicidal thoughts are almost always a symptom of depression and that suicide is almost never a rational decision. It publishes the quarterly newsletter *Surviving Suicide*, the journal *Suicide and Life-Threatening Behavior*, and fact sheets.

**American Psychiatric Association (APA)**
1000 Wilson Blvd., Ste. 1825, Arlington, VA   22209
(800) 368-5777 • fax: (707) 907-7300
e-mail: apa@psych.org
Web site: www.psych.org

An organization of psychiatrists dedicated to studying the nature, treatment, and prevention of mental disorders, the APA helps create mental health policies, distributes information about psychiatry, and promotes psychiatric research and education. It publishes the *American Journal of Psychiatry* monthly and a variety of books and newsletters.

## American Psychological Association (APA)
750 First St. NE, Washington, DC   20002-4242
(202) 336-5500 • fax: (202) 336-5708
e-mail: public.affairs@apa.org
Web site: www.apa.org

The American Psychological Association is the largest scientific and professional organization representing psychology in the United States and is the world's largest association of psychologists. It publishes numerous books, journals, and videos.

## Canadian Mental Health Association (CMHA)
180 Dundas Street West, Suite 2301
Toronto, Ontario   M5G 1Z8
  Canada
(416) 484-7750 • fax: (416) 484-4617
e-mail: info@cmha.ca
Web site: www.cmha.ca

The Canadian Mental Health Association is one of the oldest voluntary organizations in Canada. Its programs are designed to assist people suffering from mental illness find the help needed to cope with crises, regain confidence, and return to their communities, families, and jobs. It publishes books, reports, policy statements, and pamphlets.

## Children and Adults with Attention-Deficit/ Hyperactivity Disorder (CHADD)
8181 Professional Place, Ste. 150, Landover, MD   20785
(800) 233-4050 • fax (301) 306-7090
e-mail: national@chadd.org
Web site: www.chadd.org

CHADD is a nonprofit organization founded by a group of concerned parents that works to improve the lives of children and adults with attention-deficit/hyperactivity disorder through education, advocacy, and support. It publishes the quarterly *Attention!* magazine, books, and many fact sheets about the disorder.

## Citizens Commission on Human Rights (CCHR)

6616 Sunset Blvd., Los Angeles, CA   90028
(800) 869-2247 • fax (323) 467-3720
e-mail: humanrights@cchr.org
Web site: www.cchr.org

CCHR is a nonprofit organization whose goal is to expose and eradicate criminal acts and human rights abuses by psychiatry. The organization believes that psychiatric drugs cause insanity and violence. CCHR, which was founded in 1969 by the Church of Scientology, publishes numerous books, including *Psychiatry: Destroying Morals* and *Psychiatry: Education's Ruin.*

## False Memory Syndrome Foundation

1955 Locust St., Philadelphia, PA   19103
(214) 940-1040 • fax: (215) 940-1042
e-mail: mail@fmsfonline.org
Web site: www.fmsfonline.org

The foundation was established to combat False Memory Syndrome (FMS), a condition in which patients are led by their therapists to "remember" traumatic incidents—usually childhood sexual abuses—that never actually occurred. The foundation seeks to assist the victims of FMS and people falsely accused of committing child sexual abuse through publicity, counseling, and research. It publishes the FMS Foundation Newsletter and distributes information and articles on FMS.

## The International Foundation for Research and Education on Depression (iFred)

2017-D Renard Ct., Annapolis, MD   21401
(410) 268-0044 • fax: (443) 782-0739
e-mail: info@ifred.org
Web site: www.ifred.org

The International Foundation for Research and Education is an organization dedicated to researching causes of depression, to supporting those dealing with depression, and to combating stigma associated with depression.

# International Society for the Study of Dissociation (ISSD)

8201 Greensboro Drive, Suite 300, McLean, VA   22102

(703) 610-9037 • fax: (703) 610-9005

e-mail: issd@issd.org

Web site: www.issd.org

The society's membership comprises mental health professionals and students interested in dissociation. It conducts research and promotes improved understanding of this condition. It publishes the quarterly journal *Dissociation* and a quarterly newsletter.

# Mental Health America

2000 N. Beauregard Street, 6th Floor, Alexandria, VA   22311

(800) 433-5959 • fax: (703) 684-5968

Web site: www.nmha.org

Mental Health America (formerly known as the National Mental Health Association) is a consumer advocacy organization concerned with combating mental illness and improving mental health. It promotes research into the treatment and prevention of mental illness, monitors the quality of care provided to the mentally ill, and provides educational materials on mental illness and mental health. It publishes the monthly newsletter the *Bell* as well as books and pamphlets on understanding and overcoming mental illness.

# National Alliance for the Mentally Ill (NAMI)

2107 Wilson Blvd., Ste. 300, Arlington, VA   22201

(703) 524-7600 • fax: (703) 524-9094

e-mail: info@nami.org

Web site: www.nami.org

NAMI is a consumer advocacy and support organization composed largely of family members of people with severe mental illnesses such as schizophrenia, manic-depressive illness, and depression. The alliance adheres to the position that severe mental illnesses are biological brain diseases and that mentally ill people should not be blamed or stigmatized for their condition. Its publications include the bimonthly newsletter *NAMI Advocate* and the book *Breakthroughs in Antipsychotic Medications.*

## National Alliance for Research on Schizophrenia and Depression (NARSAD)

60 Cutter Mill Rd., Ste. 404, Great Neck, NY  11021
(800) 829-8289 • fax: (516) 487-6930
e-mail: info@narsad.org
Web site: www.narsad.org

The alliance is a nonprofit coalition of citizens' groups that raises funds for research into the causes, treatments, cures, and prevention of severe mental illnesses. It publishes *NARSAD Research*, a quarterly newsletter.

## National Association for Rural Mental Health (NARMH)

1756 74⁰ Avenue So., Ste. 101, Saint Cloud, MN  56301
(320) 202-1820 • fax: (320) 202-1833
e-mail: narmh@facts.ksu.edu
Web site: www.narmh.org

The association consists of mental health professionals, administrators, and other people dedicated to improving mental health services in rural areas. It provides training to mental health practitioners, and it promotes the use of mental health services by those living in rural communities. NARMH publishes the quarterly *Rural Community Health Newsletter* and distributes occasional position statements.

## National Association of Psychiatric Health Systems (NAPHS)

701 13th Street NW, Suite 950, Washington, DC  20005-3903
(202) 393-6700 • fax: (202) 783-6041
e mail: naphs@naphs.org
Web site: www.naphs.org

The association represents the interests of private psychiatric hospitals, residential treatment centers, and programs partially consisting of hospital care. It provides a forum for ideas concerning the administration, care, and treatment of the mentally ill. It publishes various fact sheets, policy recommendations, and advocate information, including *How You Can Help Reform Mental Health: A Grassroots Guide to Political Action.*

## National Institute of Mental Health (NIMH)
6001 Executive Boulevard, Room 8184, MSC 9663
Bethesda, MD   20892-9663
(301) 443-4513 • (fax) 301 443-4279
e-mail: nimhinfo@nih.gov
Web site: www.nimh.nih.gov

NIMH is the federal agency concerned with mental health research. It plans and conducts a comprehensive program of research relating to the causes, prevention, diagnosis, and treatment of mental illnesses. It produces various informational publications on mental disorders and their treatment.

## Obsessive-Compulsive Foundation (OCF)
676 State St., New Haven, CT   06511
(203) 401-2070 • fax: (203) 401-2076
e-mail: info@ocfoundation.org
Web site: www.ocfoundation.org

The foundation consists of individuals with obsessive-compulsive disorders (OCDs), their friends and families, and the professionals who treat them. It works to increase public awareness of and discover a cure for obsessive-compulsive disorders. It publishes the bimonthly *OCD Newsletter* and the pamphlet *OCD Questions and Answers.*

## SA\VE—Suicide Awareness\Voices of Education
9001 E. Bloomington Fwy, Suite #150
Bloomington, MN   55420
(952) 946-7998
Web site: www.save.org

The mission of SA\VE is to educate about suicide prevention and to speak for suicide survivors. It publishes the reports "What to Do If Someone You Know Becomes Suicidal" and "Q & A on Depression."

# Bibliography

## Books

| | |
|---|---|
| Nancy C. Andreasen | *Brave New Brain; Conquering Mental Illness in the Era of the Genome.* New York: Oxford University Press, 2001. |
| Aaron T. Beck | *Cognitive Therapy of Personality Disorders, Second Edition.* New York: Guilford, 2004. |
| Henry Emmons and Rachel Kranz | *The Chemistry of Joy: A Three-Step Program for Overcoming Depression Through Western Science and Eastern Wisdom.* New York: Fireside, 2006. |
| Ellsworth L. Fersch | *Thinking About the Insanity Defense: Answers to Frequently Asked Questions With Case Examples.* Lincoln, NE: iUniverse, Inc., 2005. |
| William Glasser | *Warning: Psychiatry Can Be Hazardous to Your Mental Health.* New York: HarperCollins, 2003. |
| Joseph Glenmullen | *The Antidepressant Solution: A Step-by-Step Guide to Safely Overcoming Antidepressant Withdrawal, Dependence, and "Addiction."* New York: Free Press, 2005. |
| Stephen P. Hinshaw | *The Mark of Shame: Stigma of Mental Illness and an Agenda for Change.* New York: Oxford University Press, 2006. |

Lara Honos-Webb    *The Gift Of ADHD: How To Transform Your Child's Problems into Strengths.* Oakland, CA: New Harbinger, 2005.

Keith Johnsgard    *Conquering Depression and Anxiety Through Exercise.* Amherst, NY: Prometheus, 2004.

Peter D. Kramer    *Against Depression.* New York: Viking Adult, 2005.

James Lake and David Spiegel    *Complementary and Alternative Treatments in Mental Health Care.* Washington, DC: American Psychiatric, 2006.

Murray Levine    *The History and Politics of Community Mental Health.* New York: Oxford University Press, 2006.

John S. Lyons    *Redressing the Emperor: Improving Our Children's Public Mental Health System.* Westport, CT: Praeger, 2004.

Jim Robbins    *A Symphony in the Brain: The Evolution of the New Brain Wave Biofeedback.* New York: Grove, 2001.

Andrew Stoll    *The Omega-3 Connection: The Groundbreaking Antidepression Diet and Brain Program.* New York: Free Press; reprint edition, 2002.

Robert Whitaker    *Mad in America: Bad Science, Bad Medicine, and the Enduring Mistreatment of the Mentally Ill.* Amherst, NY: Perseus, 2003.

# Periodicals

Peter Aldhous    "Hyperactivity Drugs Are Out of Control; Some Children Are Misdiagnosed with ADHD, Others Go Undiagnosed. Both May Face Serious Problems," *New Scientist*, April 1, 2006.

Michael Arndt    "Rewiring the Body; First Came Pacemakers. Now Exotic Implants Are Bringing Hope to Victims of Epilepsy, Paralysis, Depression, and Other Diseases," *BusinessWeek*, March 7, 2005.

Lucy Atkins    "Catch of the Day: Should We Be Giving Our Children Fish Oil Supplements?" *Guardian* (London), October 12, 2006.

Benedict Carey    "Revisiting Schizophrenia: Are Drugs Always Needed?" *New York Times*, March 21, 2006.

John Cloud    "Happiness Isn't Normal: What's the Best Form of Psychotherapy? How Can You Overcome Sadness?" *Time*, February 13, 2006.

Jennifer Couz    "Volatile Chemistry: Children and Antidepressants," *Science*, July 23, 2004.

Joyce Davidson    "Managing Anxiety Disorders: Psychopharmacologic Treatment," *Psychiatric Times*, April 1, 2006.

Norman Doidge    "The Doctor Is Totally In. On the 150⁰ Anniversary of Freud's Birth, Science Is Proving He Was Right," *Maclean's*, May 8, 2006.

Kate Douglas, et al.    "11 Steps to a Better Brain," *New Scientist*, May 28, 2005.

Robert L. Doyle    "Diagnosis and Management of ADHD in Adults," *Psychiatric Times*, June 1, 2006.

Pete Earley    "Saving My Son," *Washingtonian*, April 2006.

Nicole Foy    "Positive Feedback? Proponents Say Brainwave Training Helps with Depression and Other Ailments. Others Remain Unconvinced," *San Antonio Express-News*, March 24, 2005.

John Gibeaut    "A Matter over MIND: The Supreme Court Is Poised to Review the Insanity Defense, an Issue That Has Confounded Courts, Psychiatrists and Lawyers." *ABA Journal*, April, 2006.

James Kingsland    "The Rise and Fall of the Wonder Drugs," *New Scientist*, July 3, 2004.

Stephen Kisely    "Involuntary Treatment Without Walls—Does It Work?" *Psychiatric Times*, September 1, 2005.

James Lake    "Integrative Management of Depressed Mood: Evidence and Treatment Guidelines," *Psychiatric Times*, November 1, 2005.

Alison Motluk          "I Want to Be Happy: A Controversial New Device for Hard-to-Treat Depression Is Stirring up Hope and Debate," *O, the Oprah Magazine*, November 2005.

Kate Murphy          "Easing Depression Without Drugs," *BusinessWeek*, May 2, 2005.

Helen Phillips          "How Life Shapes the Brainscape; From Meditation to Diet, Life Experiences Profoundly Change the Structure and Connectivity of the Brain," *New Scientist*, November 26, 2005.

Fred W. Sabb and Robert M. Bilder          "From Bench to Bedside: The Future of Neuroimaging Tools in Diagnosis and Treatment," *Psychiatric Times*, February 1, 2006.

Kathryn Schulz          "Did Antidepressants Depress Japan?" *New York Times*, August 22, 2004.

Alix Spiegel          "The Dictionary of Disorder: How One Man Revolutionized Psychiatry," *New Yorker*, January 3, 2005.

Betsy Streisand          "Treating War's Toll on the Mind," *U.S. News & World Report*, October 9, 2006.

Nutan Atre Vaidya and Michael Alan Taylor          "The DSM: Should It Have a Future?" *Psychiatric Times*, March 1, 2006.

Claudia Wallis          "The New Science of Happiness," *Time*, January 17, 2005.

# Index